A Slacker's Guide to

Teradata Fundamentals and Other Myths

Table of Contents

Introduction
Concepts 5
Teradata Account Structure 11
Space Management 13
Tools and Utilities 15

Connecting to Teradata
Teradata ODBC Configuration 17
SQL Assistant 20
BTEQ 33

Executing SQL
Explain Plan 46
Statistics 48
Table Properties 51

Database and User Accounts
Teradata User Accounts 53

Tables
Table Creation 63
Unique Primary Index 66
Non-Unique Primary Index 67
Data Distribution 69
Row and Column Limitations 71
Data Types 72

Additional Table Topics
Join Processing 77
Compression 82
Identity Columns 86
No Primary Index 89
Copy Table 90

Indexes
Secondary Indexes 93
Partitioned Primary Index 98
Join Indexes 105
Hash Indexes 116

Dates and Time

Date Handling 119

Time Data Type 125

Timestamp 126

Functions, Macros and Stored Procedures

Internal Functions 127

Macros 130

Stored Procedures 134

Transactions and Security

Transactions and Locking 139

Privileges 142

Roles 143

Data Dictionary

Database and User Information 145

Object Information 146

Index Information 148

Space and Sizing Information 148

Session Information 150

Appendix – Selected Data Dictionary Views

ALLSPACE 155

COLUMNS 156

DATABASES 158

DISKSPACE 159

INDICES 160

LOGONOFF 161

ROLEINFO 162

SESSIONINFO 163

TABLES 164

USERS 166

Introduction to Teradata

"All hope abandon ye who enter here"

— Dante Alighieri, Divine Comedy

The first exposure to Teradata many people have occurs when their boss announces that the company has decided to implement a data warehouse and has selected Teradata as the vendor. The usual response ranges from "Teradata Who?" to "What's wrong with Oracle or at least something I have heard of".

After the initial shock has worn off, the first request is usually for a copy of the Teradata documentation. A quick review of the Teradata Documentation CD reveals over a hundred manuals, most containing 200 plus pages. (As if we were really going to read manuals).

What we really want to do is go play on the system. We think, hey it's just a database, I have worked on a number of database systems already, how different can it be? We just need a starting point.

If we are a corporate overachiever we can wait to be sent to formal training or try and tackle the manual jungle. However, a true Slacker geek just wants to start typing with minimal delay.

Hopefully this book will provide that starting point. The concepts of the Teradata Database will be introduced so you can start causing havoc and become an irritant as quickly as possible.

The goal of this book is to provide an overall introduction of the critical areas that are needed to understand the Teradata environment. The first and possibly most important task is to get past the jargon of learning a new system.

If this book can inspire just a tiny bit of interest in Teradata, then maybe a little knowledge will sink in unnoticed. But be careful, we wouldn't want to tarnish our reputation as a Slacker.

Teradata Concepts

Q: "What is so special about Teradata"? I have been using Oracle, SQL Server and DB2 for many years, so why does the world need another database platform?
A: The Teradata Database Architecture was developed to support extremely large amounts of data, to provide a single data store, fault tolerance, data integrity and linear scalable growth.

The architecture includes both single-node, symmetric multi-processing (SMP) systems and multi-node massively parallel processing (MPP) systems.

Q: Well, that sounds like it came right out of a Teradata marketing pitch. Can you simplify it a little bit to show how Teradata differs from traditional database systems?
A: From an architectural standpoint, database systems such as Oracle, SQL Server and DB2 are referred to as a "Shared Disk" architecture. A high level pictorial diagram of this would look like:

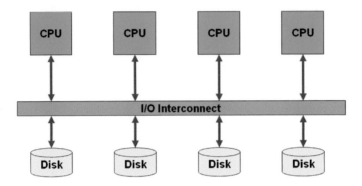

In this architecture each CPU can directly access all of the disk storage via the I/O interconnect.

Teradata, on the other hand, implements a "Shared Nothing" architecture. In this configuration each CPU processor has its own disk space allocated to it directly. This allows the CPUs the ability to work independently of each other. Information is communicated between the processors via an I/O connection. This "Shared Nothing" architecture can be represented as below:

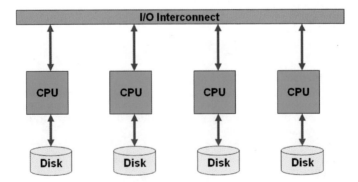

Q: Is it just the way the hardware components are connected that makes Teradata unique?
A: It is a combination of the physical architecture and the Teradata software that lets Teradata perform its magic. This design allows for Teradata to perform tasks in a Massively Parallel Processing (MPP) environment.

Q: So in your "Shared Nothing" diagram, are the CPU boxes separate individual servers? Is this what is meant when the Teradata people talk about a "node"?
A: The Teradata Database can run on a single Teradata Server which is referred to as a node. The individual server can have multiple processors and multiple cores running in a symmetric multiprocessing (SMP) architecture. The Database can be configured to run across multiple servers (nodes) connected by a high speed network link called the **BYNET.** This multi-node configuration is called a MPP (Massively Parallel Processing) and is defined as two or more SMP nodes.

Q: Many database products allow the database to be spread out over tightly coupled and loosely coupled environments. How does Teradata implement their "nodes"? Is the node the most important element of the environment?
A: Actually we need to drill down another layer to really see how the architecture is laid out. On each node there is a number of Virtual Processors that do all the real magic. There are a number of different types of these Virtual Processors (vprocs). Two of the important vpocs are the **AMP** and the **PE**. The **PE** performs session control and dispatching tasks as well as parsing functions. The **AMP** performs database functions to retrieve and update data in the database.

A key concept is that each vproc is a separate process that is isolated from the other vprocs. However they do share some resources of the SMP node such as CPU and memory.

Each node can have 127 vprocs running. There is a limit of 30,720 vprocs for an entire single system. The specific vprocs also have their own limitations for how many can be concurrently configured for each node. Communication between the vprocs is accomplished via the BYNET.

Q: You mentioned that these vprocs share resources like CPU and memory, what about the other important resource: storage?
A: Each AMP is assigned and manages a portion of the physical disk space. A pictorial representation of a node would look as follows:

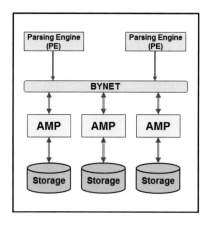

When the Teradata system is initially configured, the storage space available on the entire system is basically divided equally up among the AMPs.

Q: So unlike other database systems, like Oracle, I don't just allocate some disk files to the database and then add or remove data files later. It seems like this is going to be a lot of work figuring out what tables to assign to what AMP. Keeping the space usage balanced is going to be a nightmare!
A: No. Teradata handles storage differently than most database systems.

First, basically all of the storage space on the server is initially allocated to the Teradata Database and then that space is managed within the Database itself.

In regard to how space for tables is allocated, this is the key to Teradata's power. Teradata will manage where the rows for a table are stored. The rows for all tables will be spread across all the available AMPs automatically by the Teradata system.

Q: How does Teradata accomplish this?
A: Teradata uses a hashing algorithm to determine this row distribution. The input to the hashing function is a concept Teradata calls the **Primary Index.** *This should not be confused with the Primary Key construct used with Referential Integrity!*

Since every table is distributed across the AMPs, every table must have a Primary Index defined. It can be made up of a single column or a combination of columns.

The hashing function will always return the same result for the same value and data type. Thus, rows that have the same row hash will always go to the same AMP regardless of the table the row belongs to.

In the example shown below, the table MyPetTable has two columns; the Item_id column and the Pet_name column. The table has been created specifying that the Item_id column is the Primary Index for the table.

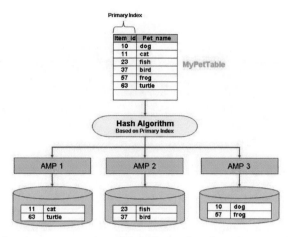

When Teradata inserts a row into this table it takes the value contained in the Item_id column and runs it through it's hashing function. The hashing function returns the number of the AMP where the row is to be stored. The AMP value returned for the row where the Pet_name column is equal to Dog is 3, so the row is stored on AMP 3.

A hash value is determined for every row contained in the table. This is how Teradata uses the Primary Index and hashing to distribute the rows of a table across all the available AMPs.

Q: So what happens if the user does not define a Primary Index when a table is created?
A: If no Primary Index is defined when the table is created, Teradata will use the first column in the table definition as the Primary Index.

Since this column may not be a good candidate for being a Primary Index, it is always a "Best Practice" to explicitly define the Primary Index.

Q: You mention that a column(s) may not be a good candidate for being a Primary Index. What makes a column(s) a good Primary Index?
A: One of the most important characteristics of a good Primary Index is that it provides an equal distribution of space across the AMPs. If our choice of a Primary Index causes us to skew the data distribution, one AMP could run out of space, while another AMP is almost empty.

Let us take a look at an example where all the values in a Primary Index hash to the same AMP. In this example, all the values in the column defined as the Primary Index are the same. This would result in all the rows being distributed to AMP 1. The remaining AMPs do not receive any rows for storage.

This data skew would cause AMP 1 to have to provide all the storage for the entire table while the remaining AMPs storage is not utilized for this table.

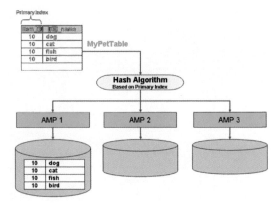

Later, we will look at additional elements that must be taken into consideration when choosing a Primary Index.

Q: Why is there all this concern about data skewing? It doesn't seem that bad to me. We can just move some additional space from the empty AMP to the AMP that is full.
A: No, we can not do that. Remember the "Shared Nothing Architecture" Teradata is based on. The AMPs each get their own equal allocation of available storage. To keep the storage space balanced, our only option is to distribute our data efficiently. The selection of a good Primary Index is how we accomplish that.

In addition, the reason Teradata is distributing the data across the AMPs is to utilize this distribution when accessing the table. By taking advantage of the power of its parallel processing architecture, each AMP can independently process data requests in parallel. An equal distribution of data is critical for this architectural design to achieve optimal overall performance.

Q: So far it seems the AMP does all the work in the Teradata database. Before we go too far and I forget, what is the purpose of the PE process?
A: The PE (parsing engine) is responsible for getting a SQL request ready to be executed and coordinating its execution. This involves the following steps:

> **Parser** – Parses the SQL into the steps required for processing
> **Optimizer** – Determines the most efficient way to process the steps
> **Generator** – Generates the code necessary to execute the process
> **Dispatcher** – Dispatches requests to the AMPs and retrieves results from the AMPs
> **Session Control** – Manages session activities (i.e. logon). Recovers from session failures.

Q: So, if I have it correct, A SQL statement is first given to one of the PEs. It is the PE's job to come up with an execution plan. The PE then makes requests to the AMPs to process the data. Once all the steps the PE identified are completed, the results are set back to whoever submitted the SQL.
A: In a simplified view, exactly!

Q: OK, so Teradata distributes the data across these AMP things. How does that help with performance?
A: Well let's look at an example; Say we want to get all of the types of pets from our sample table above. We could use a SQL statement like:

SELECT pet_name from MyPetTable;

Since, there is no WHERE clause, all the rows from the table will need to be returned. We know that the rows are spread across the AMPs, so we can easily retrieve the rows in parallel. The PE will dispatch a request to ALL-AMPS to retrieve all the required data. In this way all the AMPs are involved in accessing the data simultaneously.

Q: What is the big deal about doing a SELECT in parallel? I can do that in Oracle just by changing few parameters and adding hints to my SQL.
A: Yes you can, however in Teradata the parallelism is done at the object level and in Oracle it is basically done at the SQL level. In addition, the data for every table will be distributed and accessed in parallel without any special work. This is just part of the overall Teradata architecture.

Teradata Account Structure

Q: OK, I will give you that this Teradata scheme may, just may, be a little cool. But before I start a big argument about how my favorite database is still better than anything Teradata does, tell me a little more about how it is set up, is there a SYSTEM or SYS master account? Do I define schemas like in Oracle or databases like in SQL server? Where do I start?
A: Thanks for keeping an open mind. Teradata accounts are classified as either databases or user accounts. All of the accounts are structured in a hierarchical structure. The top account in this structure is the account called **DBC**. All other accounts are children of the DBC account.

Here is a partial account structure:

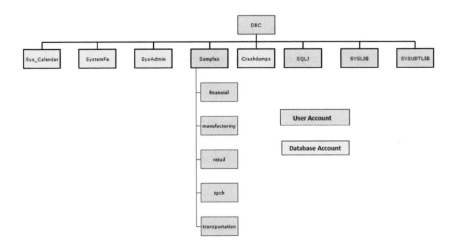

Q: Wait. Before you go any further, what is the difference between user and database accounts? In Oracle, it was always so confusing between users and schemas. What is the story here?

A: The only major difference between users and databases is that you can log into a user account. A database account can not be used to connect to the system.

Both user and database account can own objects. Either one can be parent accounts or child accounts. Database accounts can own database or user accounts and the same is true for user accounts.

Q: So DBC is the master / main account. What are some of the other accounts that are initially created when a Teradata database is first created?

A: Some of the other initial system accounts include:

User Account	Purpose
SysAdmin	The SysAdmin user account is used to store FastLoad restart control tables and views. Also stores the syntax table used to support online help.
SystemFe	System logon for the Teradata support engineer. Also used to store certain Optimizer variables.
CrashDumps	Used to store diagnostic information captured during a database memory dump.
Sys_Calendar	Contains table and views for supporting system calendar.

Q: Since the DBC account is the all powerful system account, that is what I would use as an administrator to do normal DBA tasks, Right?

A: No, DBC is a critical user on the system and we only want to log in as DBC for tasks that demand it. One issue is that the Data Dictionary for the Teradata database is owned by the user DBC and any accidental problems or issues with the Data Dictionary could have disastrous consequences.

Normally, an administrative user is created as a child of DBC. One common convention is to create a user named SysDBA for daily administration tasks. There is nothing special about this user name is called. Appropriate rights are granted from DBC so that the required administration functions can be performed by the SysDBA account.

Space Management

Q: I remember you stated that the physical space was divided up among the AMPs. How is that allocated to the users or databases? Does everyone just grab what they need?
A: First, storage is broken down into three categories in the database. We have Permanent Space (Perm Space), Spool Space and Temporary space (Temp Space). Each user can be assigned an amount of space for its use.

Q: So this assignment is like the tablespace quotas in Oracle?
A: In Oracle it is a quota, an amount of storage space that a user can not exceed. We could have five users assigned to a 1 MByte tablespace each with a quota of 1 MByte. That doesn't mean every one could create a full MByte of objects. That would require 5 Mbytes and we only physically have 1 MByte that all five users must share.

 In Teradata, Perm Space is actually assigned to that user or database. This space assignment must be given to it by another database. When a database gives an amount of their Perm Space assignment to another database, that amount is subtracted from their Perm Space. The sum of Perm Space for all the users on the system never exceeds the total Perm Space available on the system. Initially all the Perm Space is owned by DBC. From there it is distributed to the user and accounts as required. All space in a Teradata database is owned by a user or database account.

Q: How do I know how much Perm Space to assign a user? I can see if I assign too much I would be wasting space but too little and the user runs out of space. How do you track this?
A: When talking about Perm Space we look at three metrics; MaxPerm, CurrentPerm and PeakPerm. These terms indicate:

> *MaxPerm* – The maximum number of bytes available for object storage in a database or user.

> *CurrentPerm* – The number of bytes that is currently in use for object storage.

> *PeakPerm* – The largest number of bytes that was actually used for storing objects.

Q: Can an account be created without any Perm Space?
A: Sure. However, if a User or Database account is not given a Perm Space allocation they can not create any permanent objects.

Q: So what are Spool Space and Temp Space used for?
A: Spool space is used for temporary space to hold intermediate results during the execution of a SQL query. It also holds the final result set for a query. Spool space is automatically allocated and released by the system

Temp Space is used for temporary space allocated for a global temporary table. A global temporary table is a temporary table where the table definition is persistent and stored in the Data Dictionary. Only the data is temporary.

Q: Is a specific amount of Spool and Temp Space assigned to each user.
A: Actually, Spool and Temp space is controlled more like a quota. A specific amount of Spool and Temp Space can be assigned to an account but this is a limit that can not be exceeded. In addition the amount of Spool Space or Temp Space can not exceed that of its immediate parent.

Accounts "inherit" Spool and Temp Space limits from their owners.

We also classify Spool and Temp space in similar classifications as Perm Space for administration. For Spool space we have MaxSpool, CurrentSpool and PeakSpool. Similarly for Temp Space we have MaxTemp, CurrentTemp and PeakTemp

Q: Time Out! You stated earlier that all the space is owned by accounts. Where does the Spool and Temp space come from?
A: Good catch. The amount of Spool and Temp space available for use is owned or assigned to specific accounts but it is not pre-allocated. Spool and Temp space is "borrowed" from that pool of unallocated space. It is allocated automatically by the system and returned when it is no longer required.

Q: I still see a problem. What if the users have allocated their Perm Space to objects and my query needs a bunch of Spool Space. Am I dependent on other users not using all of their Perm Space allocation for my query to run correctly?
A: That could be the case but in setting up the database we can take actions to prevent that from happening. A special database can be created to help prevent this from happening. For example we could create a database called Spool_Reserve. Perm Space is allocated to this database but this account is never used to store tables. This insures that at least the amount of space assigned to Spool_Reserve is always available for Spool and Temp.

Typically, about 35% to 40% of the available space is assigned to Spool_Reserve.

Teradata Tools and Utilities

Q: What tools and utilities does Teradata provide for accessing and managing the database?
A: Teradata provides a vast array of tools and utilities to assist with the management and development of Teradata databases. Below is a sample of the most common utilities grouped somewhat by their usage.

SQL Access	
BTEQ (Basic Teradata Query)	Command line SQL query utility
Teradata SQL Assistant	Window SQL query utility
Teradata ODBC and JDBC Drivers	ODBC and JDBC drivers for accessing Teradata Database.

Database Management	
Teradata Administrator	Utility for performing database administration tasks.
Teradata Performance Monitor	Utility for monitoring performance, usage, status, contention and availability of a Teradata database.
Teradata Index Wizard	Assists with the analysis of SQL queries and workloads to suggest candidate indexes to improve performance.
Teradata Statistics Wizard	Automated method for collecting statistics or recommending statistics.
Archive/Recovery	Backup and recovery utility

Database Development	
Teradata FastExport	Utility for extracting large amounts of data from Teradata Database
Teradata FastLoad	High-performance data loading utility
Teradata MultiLoad	High-performance utility for data maintenance, including inserts, updates and deletions to table data.
Teradata TPump	Utility providing continuous update of tables.
Teradata Parallel Transporter	Load / Extract utility that combines the functionality and syntax of the utilites listed above into a single enterprise process.

These utilities will be review in greater detail in future sections.

Next Step

Q: Enough with the theory! How do I connect to a Teradata System and play?
A: In the chapters that follow, it would be benefical if you have access to a Teradata Database. Along with the topics presented, examples are included to help explain the concepts in more detail. While you can follow along with the examples provided, it will be more instructional if you can perform the examples yourself.

If you are at a site that already has implemented Teradata, contact your Teradata database administrator to see if you can get a user account created. In addition, you will need the Teradata Client Utilities installed on your computer.

On the Teradata Web site (www.teradata.com), Teradata offers a demo version of their database that runs on a Windows platform. The demo version provides an ideal environment to experiment and learn about Teradata.

Connecting to Teradata

"Data is not information, information is not knowledge, knowledge is not understanding, understanding is not wisdom."

— *Clifford Stoll*

Teradata would not be much of a database if we did not have an application that could connect to the database and execute SQL statements. As previously mentioned, there are a number of tools available for submitting SQL statements to Teradata and viewing the results. Teradata provides the BTEQ command line tool and the graphically Windows based "Teradata SQL Assistant" for handling these tasks.

In this section we will present an overview to the "Teradata SQL Assistant" utility. This is the primary tool supplied by Teradata accessing a Teradata database environment.

In addition, while learning how to utilize the utility, we will introduce a number of features useful in setting up database connections, initiating sessions and navigating through the database.

After we have completed a brief introduction to "Teradata SQL Assistant" we will take a quick look at the Teradata command line query tool BTEQ.

Teradata ODBC Configuration

Q: I completed the first section and surprisingly at least a portion of it actually made sense. So what's next?
A: I know you are chomping at the bit to start frolicking around the database but first we need look at some of the tools that are available from Teradata for interacting with the database. We are going to start with the most common tool for connecting to a Teradata database; "Teradata SQL Assistant".

"Teradata SQL Assistant" connects to the Teradata database via an ODBC connection. The Teradata specific ODBC drivers should have been installed when the Teradata client utilities was installed.

Q: Since the Teradata ODBC driver has already been installed, is everything set up ready to go?
A: Before we can make an ODBC connection to a database we need to go into the Windows ODBC Data Source Administrator and configure an ODBC Data Source for the Teradata server we want to connect to.

On the Windows Control Panel Menu, locate the Administrative Tools under System and Security. Clicking this option will display a list of tools. Select and click on the "Data Source (ODBC)" item.

The following window will be displayed:

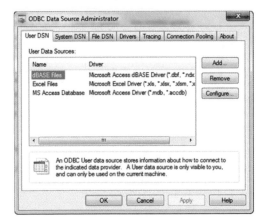

There are a number of tab pages on this window. To create the ODBC Data Source you can either user the "User DSN" page or the "System DSN" page. Defining the Data Source on the "User DSN" will make it available only to the user who creates it. Defining the DataSource on the "System DSN" page will make it available to all users who log into that computer.

Click on the "Add" button and a sub-menu will be displayed, requesting you to select the driver your Data Source will utilize. Scroll down until you find the entry for Teradata. Highlight it and then click "Finish".

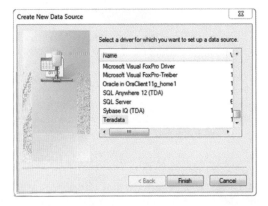

If you do not see an option for specifying Teradata it indicates that the Teardata ODBC driver has not been installed on your system. You will need to go back and install the driver.

After Teradata has been selected, the set up screen for defining a Teradata ODBC Data Source will then be displayed.

Minimally you need to provide a name for the Data Source and the Name or IP address of the Teradata server.

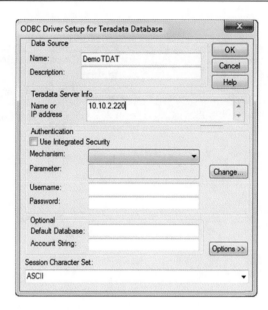

Once you have completed entering this information you can click "OK". You will then be returned to the original Administrator screen. You should now see an entry for the Data Source you just created.

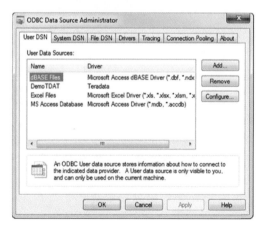

Clicking "OK" will exit the ODBC Data Source Administrator tool;

Q: I was able to create a Teradata Data Source for the database I want to connect to but I have a quick question. On the Setup Page there was an option for entering a Username and a Password. Don't I want to enter them here?
A: The ability to enter your username and password as part of the Data Source definition is provided. However from a security perspective it is never a good idea to have a password hardcoded. When you go to make a connection with the Data Source you will be prompted for the username and password.

Teradata SQL Assistant

Q: Now that I have the ODBC Data Source defined, how does this legendary application "Teradata SQL Assistant" work?
A: I am not so sure about the legendary tag but it is the standard graphical interface supplied by Teradata. "Teradata SQL Assistant" is a Microsoft Windows application that allows you to connect to any ODBC-compliant database to submit SQL statements and retrieve the results.

Let's go head and run the Teradata SQL Assistant application by clicking on:

Start > Programs > Teradata SQL Assistant

The following screen should be displayed. The various sections of the Teradata SQL Assistant application are indicated below.

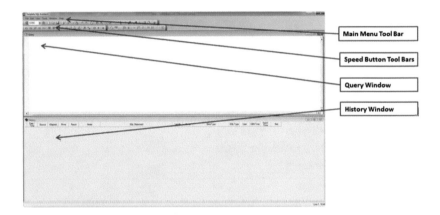

Q: Yes, I saw this before when I tested my ODBC connection in the first section. What are all the options available in Teradata SQL Assistant?
A: The Main Menu drop down tool bar provides a method to select the various options available in Teradata SQL Assistant.

File   Edit   View   Tools   Window   Help

Below illustrates the various commands available under each of the Main Menu Drop down Tool Bar options:

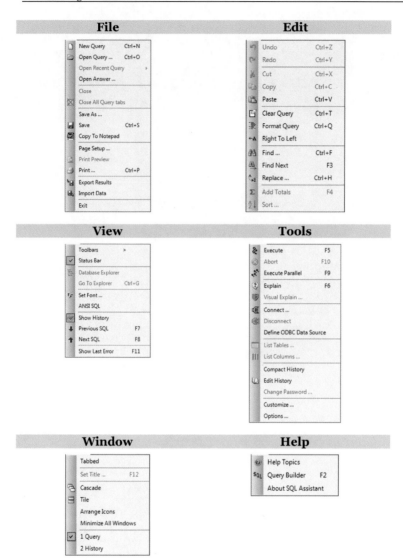

In addition, many of the commonly used commands can be invoked from Speed buttons available on the Speed Button Tool Bar.

Q: That is all well and good but how do I connect to my Teradata database?

A: On the top ribbon speed bar click on the green connector icon

This will bring up a menu to allow you to select an ODBC Data Source. On the
Machine Data Source tab page select the Data Source you defined in the
previous section.

This will then bring up a Teradata Database Connect menu. Here you can enter
your username and password and then click "OK".

**Q: Hurrah, it looks like I was able to connect to the Teradata
database successfully. However, the screen changed its layout after I
the connection was made. A new window on the left was displayed.
The title on the new window calls it the "Database Explorer". What
is the purpose of the "Database Explorer Window"?**
A: Once a successful connection is established to a Teradata database, the
"Database Explorer" window is displayed.

Below is an example of "Teradata SQL Assistant" with the "Database Explorer"
shown.

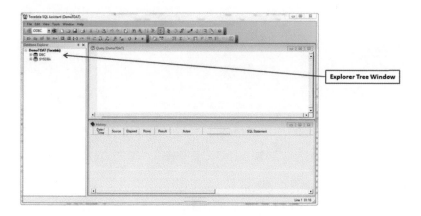

This additional new sub window is displayed showing databases and users contained in the database you are connected to.

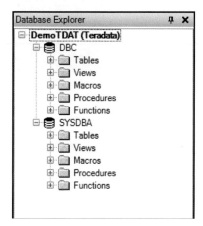

The Database Explorer Window shows a list of the database and user accounts in the database.

If you click on one of the accounts the tree will expand to list out entries for tables, views, macros, functions and procedures.

Clicking on one of these object categories will display the names of all the current type of objects.

Q: I can only see two account entries, DBC and SYSDBA. In the first section you mentioned a number of other accounts. Why are these not displayed?
A: By default all the accounts that existing in the database are not initially displayed. You must add them.

If you Right click in the Explorer window the following popup menu will be displayed

Select Add Database

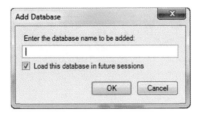

You enter the name of the database you want added to the list. If the check box on the bottom of the popup is left checked, the next time you run Teradata SQL Assistant; it will automatically be included in your list of accounts.

Enter sys_calendar and then click OK

You should now see the database sys_calendar list in your explorer tree.

Q: I clicked on the table's entry under DBC and the whole entry just went away. What happened?
A: If no objects exist under the category entry, the entry is removed after you click on it. It just means that there were no tables you had permissions to see under DBC.

Expand the entry for sys_calendar and then click on the entry for Tables. You should now see a table under sys_calendar called CALDATES.

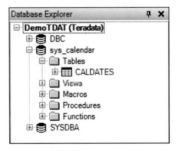

Q: I see the CALDATES table reference. What does this table contain?
A: Well, we have a number of ways to get information about tables from this point.

First, if you expand the child nodes further you can see entries for indexes and columns. Expand these entries to see that the CALDATES table has no indexes on it and it contains a single column called "cdate".

To actually look at the data, we can use Teradata SQL assistant to execute a SQL statement that displays the contents of the table.
In the Query Window enter the SQL statement:

```
select * from CALDATES
```

Now click on the "Execute" speed button. ![]

Q: I don't see any data returned. What did I do wrong?
A: We had an error in our SQL statement. While the syntax of the SQL statement was correct, Teradata will always assume that tables will exist in the default database unless you fully qualify the table name.

An error message was displayed, but since "Teradata SQL Assistant" hides it so well (in the bottom left had corner), it often goes un-detected.

Notice the information Grid in the History Window. You can see an error number in the results column. This error number can be used to look up more detailed information in the Teradata documentation. It may be worthwhile to look up this error message to become familiar with Teradata's documentation.

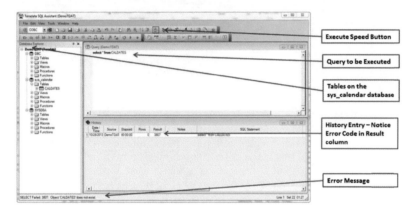

Now, we add the database name to the table name and re-execute our query.

```
select * from sys_calendar.CALDATES
```

Q: Here we go again! The query seemed to be executing but then this message box popped up with some kind on question if I want to cancel the query. What now?
A: Teradata issues a warning to the user if the result set being generated exceeds a default value. When this value is exceeded a warning is issued. This helps prevent run away queries from going on forever. If you click "No" the SQL will continue.

Clicking "Yes" will terminate the query and display the result set that has been generated to this point.

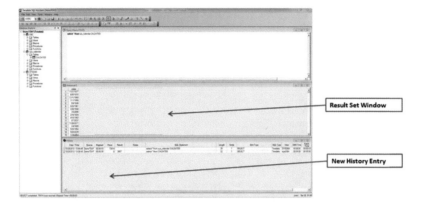

Q: I was able to generate the result set but why is the order so weird. In Oracle, if no order was specified, I would normally see the data in the order it was loaded. What I am looking at appears to be random. Why?

A: You need to remember how Teradata stores and retrieves data. Even for internal Teradata tables, the data is spread across the AMPs by the Primary Index. To execute a select, Teradata sends a request to all the AMPs to get the data that they stored that meets the criteria specified. The result set is built as the AMPs return the data. Thus, the order is determined by the speed in which the AMPs complete retrieving their data and what data was distributed to that AMP.

In Teradata, you should never assume a result set will be returned in any type of order. If the order is important include an ORDER BY clause in your SQL.

Try:

```
select * from sys_calendar.CALDATES ORDER by cdate;
```

Q: Oh those evil AMPs again! However that seems to make sense. But, I still get that error about the size of my result set. If I am just trying to get an idea what the data in a table looks like, that could be irritating. I tried adding a WHERE condition, like I do in ORACLE to limit the number of rows returned

```
select * from sys_calendar.CALDATES where rownum < 4;
```

but I got an error that rownum did not exist. Is there any way to do something similar in Teradata?

A: Of course. Teradata provides a SQL keyword to instruct the PE to only return a sub-set of the data. The keyword is SAMPLE and is followed by an integer, indicating the number of rows you want returned.

```
select * from sys_calendar.CALDATES SAMPLE 10
```

The rows returned are random rows.

Q: Going back to something you mentioned the first time I tried this SQL, what was the concept with this default database? I am guessing that when I log into Teradata, my login database is the default database but the way you phrased it appears to suggest it might not always be?
A: Good catch. Your current default database can be specified when you connect or changed at any time during your session.

To specify a default database that is different from the user database you are connecting with, you have to remember back to when you made your ODBC connection.

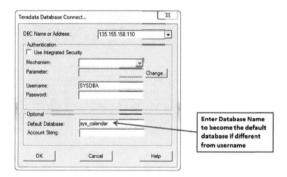

Click on the disconnect speed button and click on the connect speed button. This will bring up the ODBC connection again and select the Teradata Demo System. This time, in the Optional Section under Default Database enter the database name sys_calendar

After you are successfully connected again, let's try the same initial SQL:

```
select * from CALDATES
```

Now it works without the table name being fully qualified.

While in a Teradata session, we can also change the current database to something different with the SQL command:

```
DATABASE SysDBA;
```

Executing this command will change our default database to SysDBA. If we tried to execute the SQL above that is not fully qualified we would get our "table does not exist error message" again.

Q: Before we go any further, I had a question I forgot to ask when we were configuring our ODBC data source. On the Driver Options menu, there was an option to select "Session Mode". I have heard

people talk about "Teradata Mode" and "ANSI Mode". What is this all about?

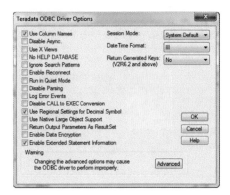

A: A session connected to Teradata can execute in either ANSI mode or Teradata Mode. There are a number of subtle differences between the two modes which we will point out as we go along.

One of the first differences is that in TERADATA mode transactions are committed immediately unless they are part of a BEGIN TRANACTION .. END TRANSACTION block.

In ANSI mode transactions are not committed until a COMMIT statement is executed. Thus, BEGIN TRANSACTION and END TRANSACTION statements are not valid in ANSI mode and COMMIT is not valid in TERADATA mode.

There will be other differences but in general ANSI mode insures that actions on the database confirm to the ANSI standards. Since ANSI mode is a newer addition to TERADATA, utilizing TERADATA mode will insure compatibility to older versions of the Teradata database.

Q: Hopefully, that will become clearer as we proceed. I went back and re-ran the CALDATES select SQL and then went to File > Export Results in the Main Menu Tool Bar. When I selected it nothing happened. Where did it export the results to?
A: It hasn't exported anything yet. The option acts as a toggle.
Shown below is the "Teradata SQL Assistant" screen with the location of the "Export Results" option selection and the message to indicate that you are in export mode.

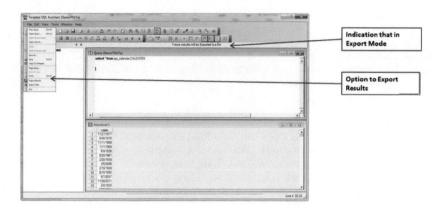

Re-execute you SQL select statement now that you have selected the option. With the Export Results option being set we now get an open file dialog box being displayed. You can specify the format, file name and location for the result set data to be exported.

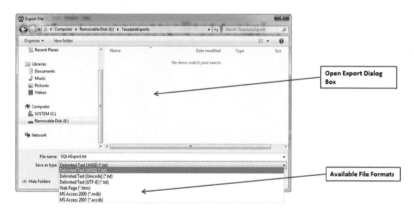

Q: So I have to decide before I run my query if I want to export the results? That or re-run the query again?
A: Unfortunately yes. Just for practice go ahead and export the result set for part of the CALDATES table. Save the export file we will use it later.

Q: Well that seems rather "user un-friendly"! I guess I shouldn't complain, at least the export of the result set data worked. I am almost afraid to ask: "Can save my SQL text?" Please tell me that is not a big problem.
A: Luckily, that is pretty straight forward. Just select the "Save As" option under the File drop down of the Main Menu Tool Bar (or use the Speed Button). A Save Dialog Window will appear. Specify a directory and a name and then click on the Save button. Your SQL text will be saved.

Save you CALDATES SQL select statement to a file in a directory on your machine.

Now change the SQL statement and remove the SAMPLE portion of the SQL statement.

Now select the "Open Query" option under the File drop down of the Main Menu Tool Bar (or use the Speed Button). Select the CALDATES file we just saved and click the Open button.

The query we previously saved is now in our Query Window.

Q: I am glad to see I can save and load SQL from text files but what happened to my existing SQL (the one I modified by removing the SAMPLE clause). The window just disappeared. SQL Assistant didn't even ask me if I wanted to save it first. How do I open multiple Query Windows at one time?
A: You actually did just create multiple Query Windows. If you look closely the Query window is now a tabbed page. You now have two tabs in the Query Window. One has the modified query and the other has the query loaded from the SQL file.

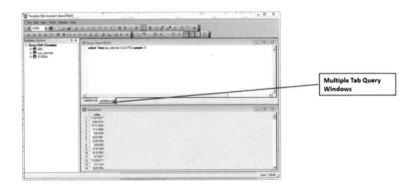

Q: If I can have multiple Query Windows open at one time, can I have multiple Result Set windows open also?
A: Yes. By default Teradata SQL Assistant closes the open Result Set windows whenever a new query is run. This can be turned off so that Result Set Windows from previous queries will remain open until you close them.

To select this option go to the Options selection under the Tools heading of the Main Menu Tool Bar.

Navigate to the AnswerSet option page.

Clear the check box marked "Close answer windows before submitting new query".

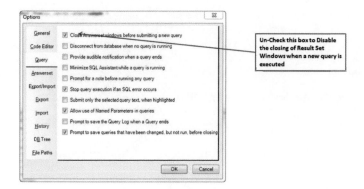

Now a Result Set window will remain visible until you explicitly close it.

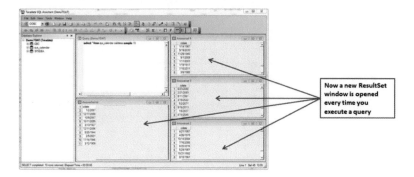

Q: Is there anything additional I can do with the result sets?
A: Actually there are some additional features that are kind of nice. Under the File drop down of the Main Menu Tool Bar select the "Open Answer ..." selection. When the "Open Answer Set" dialog box is displayed, select the file you saved from before. Click the Open button.

The result set you previous stored has now been re-loaded. It is a nice feature that allows you to save a result set and then be able to reload the result data back into "Teradata SQL Assistant".

You can close an Answerset Window by clicking the 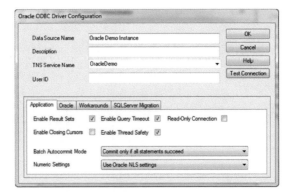 button in the upper right corner or after highlighting the window using the "Close" option under the "File" File heading of the Main Menu Tool Bar. There is also an option under the "File" heading to close all of the open AnswerSets by selecting the "Close all AnswerSets" option.

Q: I think I have the basics of Teradata SQL assistant. I will need to play around with it to get some more experience but it seems somewhat straight forward. One more quick question. What is the difference between the ⬚ button and the ⬚ button when executing a SQL query?

A: When you select the Execute button (the single set of foot steps) each SQL is sent to the database to be executed as individual entities. The Execute Parallel button (set of multiple footsteps) sends the entire SQL text to the database as a single request. This way the database can execute multiple statements at the same time. For now use the Execute option.

Q: Any other incredible things you care to mention about Teradata SQL Assistant?

A: Well, I don't know how incredible it is but it is interesting. Teradata SQL Assistant will actually work with any ODBC compliant database connection.

If you create an ODBC DSN configuration using the Oracle ODBC Driver to an Oracle Database instance you have access to, Teradata SQL Assistant can make a connection to the Oracle Database.

Start Teradata SQL Assistant and click on the connect button. Instead of selecting the Teradata Data Source, select the Oracle Demo Instance entry. You should then be prompted for your username and password.

After you enter your login information, you should now be able to access Oracle instance with Teradata SQL Assistant.

Try to execute a SQL statement to retrieve data from a table you have access to in the Oracle Instance.

As was mentioned when we first reviewed the features of Teradata SQL Assistant, it can be used to connect to any ODBC compliant database.

This can be a useful option if you need to work in Teradata and Oracle simultaneously.

BTEQ

Q: Does Teradata provide any other tools other than Teradata SQL Assistant for accessing a Teradata database? What about something similar to SQL Plus in Oracle?
A: Yes, Teradata provides a command level interface to the database called BTEQ. BTEQ stands for Basic Teradata Query. While BTEQ is a non-graphical tool, it can provide a number of important features not found in its graphical cousin. These unique features include; running on various platforms including Unix and Linux as well as Windows, creating script files, commands to assist with handling exceptions and controlling execution and allowing for the import and export of data.

Another difference from many other query tools, including "Teradata SQL Assistant" is that BTEQ does not interface to the database using ODBC. It makes a direct connection to the Teradata database using the Teradata CLI interface.

A number of the Teradata options, such as formatting, are also available only in BTEQ. In Teradata SQL Assistant and other ODBC based tools, these options are not available because they do not conform to the ODBC specification.

Q: Sounds interesting. How do I go about using BTEQ?
A: Bring up a command prompt window by navigating to:

Start > All Programs > Accessories > Command Prompt

In the window that comes up enter **BTEQ** at the prompt:

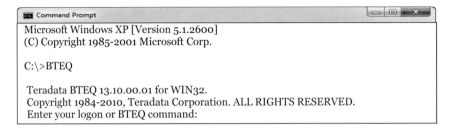

All BTEQ commands begin with a period. To get in and out of BTEQ we use:

> **.LOGON**
> **.LOGOFF**
> **.EXIT**

To logon on to our demo database use the following syntax:
> *.logon tpid/username*

The *tpid* identifies the Teradata server, for our demo database the tpid is DemoDTAT. In the examples here we will use the user account sysDBA but you can substitute your user name instead.

> .logon DEMOTDAT/sysDBA

You will then be prompted to enter your password. After entering a valid password, you should be connected to the database.

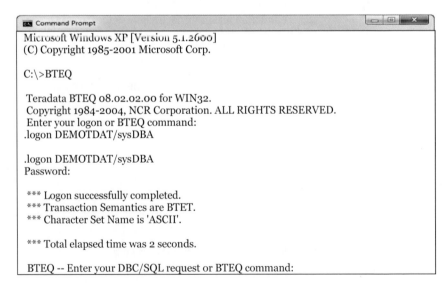

Q: Houston we have a problem. My logon failed. I got the following weird error message when I tried to logon.

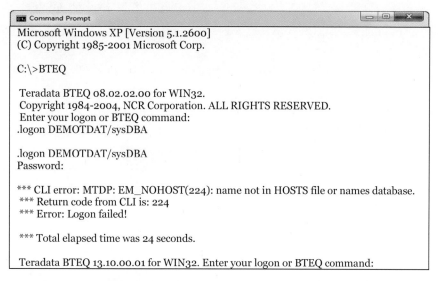

Microsoft Windows XP [Version 5.1.2600]
(C) Copyright 1985-2001 Microsoft Corp.

C:\>BTEQ

Teradata BTEQ 08.02.02.00 for WIN32.
Copyright 1984-2004, NCR Corporation. ALL RIGHTS RESERVED.
Enter your logon or BTEQ command:
.logon DEMOTDAT/sysDBA

.logon DEMOTDAT/sysDBA
Password:

*** CLI error: MTDP: EM_NOHOST(224): name not in HOSTS file or names database.
*** Return code from CLI is: 224
*** Error: Logon failed!

*** Total elapsed time was 24 seconds.

Teradata BTEQ 13.10.00.01 for WIN32. Enter your logon or BTEQ command:

A: That's what we get for assuming that everything was set up correctly. The problem is that BTEQ could not translate the server name DEMOTDAT into a correct IP address. One method to resolve this issue would be to connect by specifying the IP address directly.
In this example we substitute the actual IP address of our Teradata server, in this case 10.10.2.220 for the DEMODTAT name previously specified.

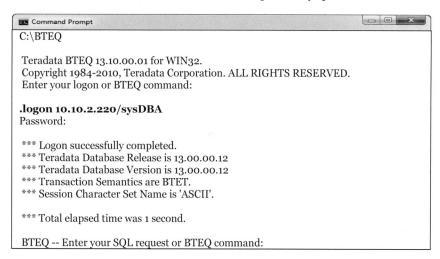

C:\BTEQ

Teradata BTEQ 13.10.00.01 for WIN32.
Copyright 1984-2010, Teradata Corporation. ALL RIGHTS RESERVED.
Enter your logon or BTEQ command:

.logon 10.10.2.220/sysDBA
Password:

*** Logon successfully completed.
*** Teradata Database Release is 13.00.00.12
*** Teradata Database Version is 13.00.00.12
*** Transaction Semantics are BTET.
*** Session Character Set Name is 'ASCII'.

*** Total elapsed time was 1 second.

BTEQ -- Enter your SQL request or BTEQ command:

Q: That works but surely there must be a way to associate the name of the Teradata Database Server with its IP address.
A: Yes, there indeed is a way for you to make this association on your own workstation if your network administration has not defined it globally.

Typically, the network administrator configures the network to allow the translation of the Teradata Database Server name into the corresponding IP address. However, this can also be done locally on your own client workstation.

The **hosts** file is used by your local workstation to also provide this translation ability.

On a Windows machine, use Windows Explorer to navigate to:

C:\WINDOWS\system32\drivers\etc

Open the file "hosts" using Notepad and add the line indicated below.

```
hosts - Notepad
File  Edit  Format  View  Help
# Copyright (c) 1993-1999 Microsoft Corp.
#
# This is a sample HOSTS file used by Microsoft TCP/IP for Windows.
#
# This file contains the mappings of IP addresses to host names. Each
# entry should be kept on an individual line. The IP address should
# be placed in the first column followed by the corresponding host name.
# The IP address and the host name should be separated by at least one
# space.
#
# Additionally, comments (such as these) may be inserted on individual
# lines or following the machine name denoted by a '#' symbol.
#
# For example:
#
#      102.54.94.97     rhino.acme.com          # source server
#       38.25.63.10     x.acme.com              # x client host

127.0.0.1       localhost
10.10.2.220     DemoTDATcop1
```

Q: So I tried to logon again using the server name I entered in the hosts file (.logon DemoTDATcop1/sysDBA) but I am still getting the same error. What am I doing wrong now?
A: In Teradata the actual server name is referred to as the TDPID or Teradata Director Program Id. The TDPID is actually composed of 2 parts <hostname><node>. The node is usually referred to as cop1, cop2, ... This can be used for load balancing of connections in a Teradata environment. When using BTEQ we only specify the <hostname> portion.

```
Command Prompt
C:\BTEQ

Teradata BTEQ 13.10.00.01 for WIN32.
Copyright 1984-2010, Teradata Corporation. ALL RIGHTS RESERVED.
Enter your logon or BTEQ command:

.logon DemoTDAT/sysDBA
Password:

*** Logon successfully completed.
*** Teradata Database Release is 13.00.00.12
*** Teradata Database Version is 13.00.00.12
*** Transaction Semantics are BTET.
```

```
*** Session Character Set Name is 'ASCII'.

*** Total elapsed time was 1 second.

BTEQ -- Enter your SQL request or BTEQ command:
```

Q: Now that I have successfully connected to the Teradata Database it might be good to know how to get out of BTEQ before I start causing trouble.
A: To logoff you can simply type: *.LOGOFF* which will end your session but not exit the BTEQ application. This would allow you to connect to another database or logon with a different user name. If you just wanted to exit the application you can use *.EXIT*

Q: Thanks, it is always good to know how to exit an application cleanly. So now can I just enter and execute SQL like I did in Teradata SQL Assistant?
A: To execute a SQL command you simply need to enter the SQL text and hit "Enter". The query will be executed and the results returned to your command window. You **do not** prefix your SQL command with a period like you do for BTEQ commands and you must end the SQL text with a semi-colon. Your SQL statement can span multiple lines with the semi-colon at the end of a line telling BTEQ to go ahead and execute the command.

Using a simple SQL select query, let's execute it using BTEQ.

Type:

select * from sys_calendar.CALDATES SAMPLE 5;

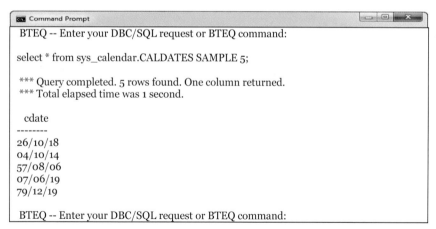

```
BTEQ -- Enter your DBC/SQL request or BTEQ command:

select * from sys_calendar.CALDATES SAMPLE 5;

*** Query completed. 5 rows found. One column returned.
*** Total elapsed time was 1 second.

 cdate
--------
26/10/18
04/10/14
57/08/06
07/06/19
79/12/19

BTEQ -- Enter your DBC/SQL request or BTEQ command:
```

Q: That works fine but typically using a command line interface I tend to want to execute long SQLs or a number of SQL statements all at once. Can I put the SQL commands in a text file and then have BTEQ execute it from there?

A: Of course. First we create a text file with the SQL commands we want to execute. For this example we will save the file as BTEQscript.txt

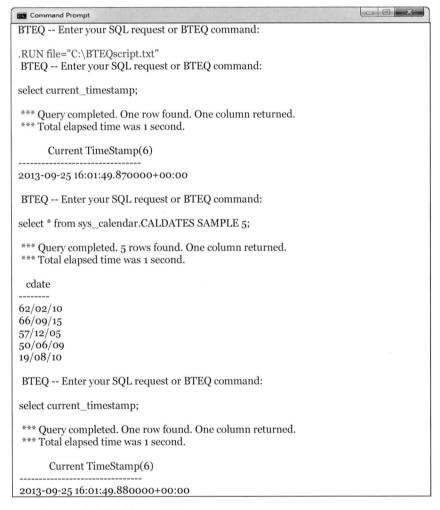

```
BTEQscript.txt - Notepad
File  Edit  Format  View  Help
select current_timestamp;
select * from sys_calendar.CALDATES SAMPLE 5;
select current_timestamp;
```

Then within BTEQ we can use the .RUN command to read that file and have BTEQ execute the SQL.

```
Command Prompt
BTEQ -- Enter your SQL request or BTEQ command:

.RUN file="C:\BTEQscript.txt"
BTEQ -- Enter your SQL request or BTEQ command:

select current_timestamp;

*** Query completed. One row found. One column returned.
*** Total elapsed time was 1 second.

      Current TimeStamp(6)
------------------------------
2013-09-25 16:01:49.870000+00:00

BTEQ -- Enter your SQL request or BTEQ command:

select * from sys_calendar.CALDATES SAMPLE 5;

*** Query completed. 5 rows found. One column returned.
*** Total elapsed time was 1 second.

   cdate
--------
62/02/10
66/09/15
57/12/05
50/06/09
19/08/10

BTEQ -- Enter your SQL request or BTEQ command:

select current_timestamp;

*** Query completed. One row found. One column returned.
*** Total elapsed time was 1 second.

      Current TimeStamp(6)
------------------------------
2013-09-25 16:01:49.880000+00:00
```

So we can see BTEQ executes each command from the file just as if it was directly entered into BTEQ.

Q: When I created by text file I happened to put the semi-colons at the beginning of the line.

```
select current_timestamp
;select * from sys_calendar.CALDATES SAMPLE 5
;select current_timestamp;
```

Why does my output look different?

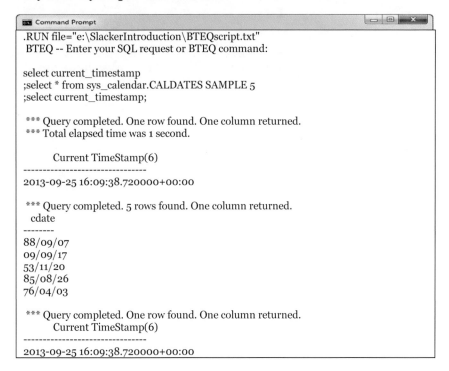

```
.RUN file="e:\SlackerIntroduction\BTEQscript.txt"
BTEQ -- Enter your SQL request or BTEQ command:

select current_timestamp
;select * from sys_calendar.CALDATES SAMPLE 5
;select current_timestamp;

*** Query completed. One row found. One column returned.
*** Total elapsed time was 1 second.

       Current TimeStamp(6)
-------------------------------
2013-09-25 16:09:38.720000+00:00

*** Query completed. 5 rows found. One column returned.
  cdate
--------
88/09/07
09/09/17
53/11/20
85/08/26
76/04/03

*** Query completed. One row found. One column returned.
       Current TimeStamp(6)
-------------------------------
2013-09-25 16:09:38.720000+00:00
```

A: The placement of the semi-colon is actually very important. When BTEQ sees a semi-colon at the end of a line it assumes that everything before it should be submitted to the database for execution. When you placed the semi-colons at the beginning of the line, BTEQ submitted all three of your SQL statements to the Teradata database to be executed at the same time.

In the first example, notice the two timestamps that were displayed are slightly different. In the second example, they are exactly the same. This is because in the first example the three SQLs were executed serially, however in the second example they were executed in parallel.

Q: Speaking of scheduling, in the examples shown so far, we first logged into BTEQ at the command line and then run the queries from our file. Can we script the entire login process into a single file

to make it easier to schedule via "Windows Task Scheduler" or CRON?
A: Sure, as shown below we can include the .logon and .logoff commands in our script file. However we will have to include the password on the .logon command line.

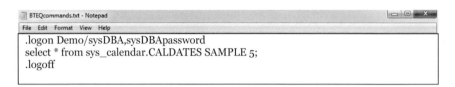

After creating our script we can run BTEQ and redirect BTEQ to read from the file you created instead of from the terminal. We do this by using the command "BTEQ < ScriptFileName.txt".

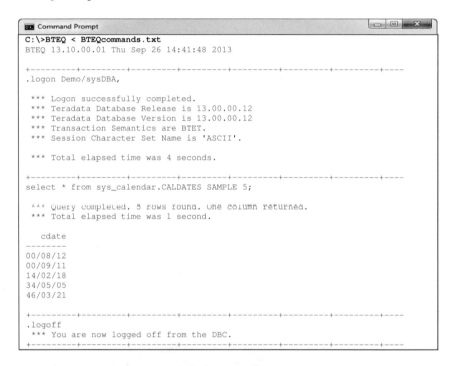

Q: BTEQ looks like is can provide a good mechanism for scripting SQL statements that are executed frequently. This would especially be true for administration tasks. Where else can BTEQ be useful?
A: BTEQ has a huge breath of features that can be of great beneficial to the user. One useful feature is the ability to format the results from a SQL query into a report format. Here is a simple example of a BTEQ script that selects information about tables and formats it in a report format.

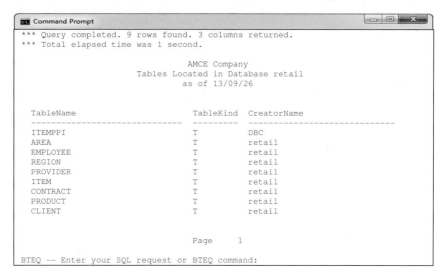

When we execute these BTEQ commands we get the following result.

This can be very useful for creating adhoc reports that can be easily scheduled.

Q: Yes, it definitely makes a report easier to read and look more professional when it is formatted nicely. Extracting data from a Teradata database into a formatted report is an excellent option of BTEQ but what if I need to extract data from one Teradata database and move it to another Teradata Database? Does BTEQ export and import features provide a way to accomplish this?

A: BTEQ provides a number of options for importing and exporting data. One reason this might prove useful is to move data from one Teradata database to another The .export BTEQ command allows for the ability to extract data from a table and save these results to a file.

First we can use the .EXPORT command tell BTEQ to store the results from subsequent SQL statements into a file. Below we instruct BTEQ to save the SQL results into the file SampleExport.txt. We then execute a SQL select statement to retrieve all the data from the InputData table. Finally we use the .EXPORT RESET command to close the export file.

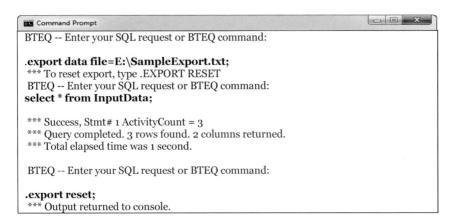

On the Teradata database where we want to load the data, the .IMPORT command specifies the name of the file which contains the data. We then use an SQL insert statement to insert the data into our destination LoadData table. A .REPEAT statement is used to loop through all the rows of data extracted.

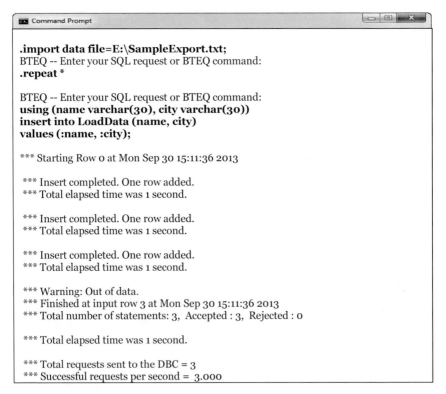

Q: Within a script is there a way I can control what happens when an error occurs?

A: BTEQ includes a number of commands for testing error codes and altering the execution of statements in the script. The .IF command can test error codes from previously executed SQL statements and jump over statements if necessary.

In the example below we try to execute a SQL statement that we know is going to fail. After the SQL statement fails, we include the .IF statement to jump over the .EXIT statement.

```
Command Prompt                                          ─  □  X
select * from TableDoesNotExists;
 *** Failure 3807 Object 'TableDoesNotExists' does not exist.
             Statement# 1, Info =0
 *** Total elapsed time was 1 second.


 BTEQ -- Enter your SQL request or BTEQ command:
.IF errorcode = 3807 THEN .GOTO NoTable

.IF errorcode = 3807 THEN .GOTO NoTable
.GOTO NoTable
 BTEQ -- Enter your SQL request or BTEQ command:
.EXIT

.EXIT
 *** Skipped.
 BTEQ -- Enter your SQL request or BTEQ command:
.LABEL NoTable

.LABEL NoTable
 BTEQ -- Enter your SQL request or BTEQ command:
select 'We came here because of error';

select 'We came here because of error';

 *** Query completed. One row found. One column returned.
 *** Total elapsed time was 1 second.

'We came here because of error'
-------------------------------
We came here because of error

 BTEQ -- Enter your SQL request or BTEQ command:
.EXIT

.EXIT
 *** You are now logged off from the DBC.
 *** Exiting BTEQ...
 *** RC (return code) = 8
```

Q: Except when I needed to create a SQL script, is there any other reason I would want to be so retro as to go back to using a command line utility?
A: Actually, in some cases "Teradata SQL Assistant" can become out of sync with the database. Although it is rare, it have been observed that issues can arise when an error occurs during the execution of a SQL submitted from "Teradata SQL Assistant". SQL Assistant appears to still be executing the SQL but if you look at the session from the database, the session is idle. SQL Assistant is basically locked up. Worse yet, you never see the error message that caused the problem.

This condition is seen primarily when executing long running SQLs. The problem is related to the ODBC connection. Since BTEQ does not use ODBC it does not exhibit this problematic behavior. BTEQ is the tool of choice for this type of SQL execution.

Q: Well I may have to rethink my distain for command line tools. BTEQ truly has a lot of depth with all the features it provides.
A: This was just a quick overview of the power that BTEQ can offer. BTEQ has a lot more to offer than what was covered here. If this introduction sparked interested, you could always go totally crazy and break out the "Basic Teradata Query Reference" manual for a little lite reading.

Executing SQL

"Why has elegance found so little following? That is the reality of it. Elegance has the disadvantage, if that's what it is, that hard work is needed to achieve it and a good education to appreciate it."

— *Edsger Dijkstra*

Now that we have introduced the basic concepts of a Teradata database and reviewed how to connect and execute a few basic SQL statements with "Teradata SQL Assistant", we can dive deeper into some of the Teradata database particulars.

To get started, in this chapter we will look at some of the overall specific details of working in a Teradata environment.

Q: After guiding me through making a connection to Teradata, I tried to run a simple query to see the current date. I executed "select sysdate from dual" in Teradata SQL Assistant and got an error. What is the problem? I cannot imagine getting any simpler than that?
A: You are still trying to use Oracle syntax and concepts in Teradata and many of these options are not valid in a Teradata environment. The functionality is usually there however the syntax may be different. Remember, Teradata tries to follow the ANSI standards.

Teradata does not have the dual table concept. To select a constant in Teradata you can simply leave off the FROM clause.

Also, sysdate is a Oracle specific reserved word. In Teradata you can either user DATE or the more ANSI standard option of CURRENT_DATE.

```
select current_date
Current Date
11/14/2013
```

Q: I understand that the syntax may be a little different in Teradata. However, I would assume that as far as basic SQL operations go, Teradata would be similar to all the other databases out there. What specifics should I look out for?
A: In order to review some Teradata specifics, let us first create a simple table to use in our examples. We will talk about Teradata tables later in excruciating detail but for now just execute the following SQL.

```
CREATE SET TABLE Months
    (Month_Id    INTEGER,
     Description VARCHAR(50) )
PRIMARY INDEX ( Month_Id );
```

While the syntax for the CREATE TABLE command is similar to other database system, the PRIMARY INDEX clause is unique to Teradata. We briefly discussed the PRIMARY INDEX earlier and it will be a continuous topic throughout our trek. However, for now just create the table with the SQL statement shown.

The table can now be queried and the results reviewed.

```
select * from Months
Month_Id  Description
....... No Rows Returned
```

Explain Plan

Q: Of course no rows were returned. We just created the table and nothing was inserted. What did we learn from that?
A: Not much except we verified that the table was created correctly and that it is empty.

Using such a simple query, we may not think much about the exact steps Teradata used to execute our query but in more complicated cases it could prove extremely useful.

Teradata provides the ability to generate an English like description of the steps it will take to execute a query. The EXPLAIN statement provides this functionality.

EXPLAIN ⟶ SQL Statement ⟶ ;

First we can insert some data into our Months table.

```
insert into Months values (1, 'January');
insert into Months values (2,'February');
insert into Months values (3,'March');
insert into Months values (4,'April');
insert into Months values (5,'May');
insert into Months values (6,'June');
insert into Months values (7,'July');
insert into Months values (8,'August');
insert into Months values (9,'September');
insert into Months values (10,'October');
insert into Months values (11,'November');
insert into Months values (12,'December');
```

Now we execute an EXPLAIN on the simple SQL .

```
EXPLAIN select * from months
1) First, we lock a distinct SYSDBA."pseudo table" for read on a
   RowHash to prevent global deadlock for SYSDBA.months.
2) Next, we lock SYSDBA.months for read.
3) We do an all-AMPs RETRIEVE step from SYSDBA.months by way of an
   all-rows scan with no residual conditions into Spool 1
   (group_amps), which is built locally on the AMPs.  The size of
   Spool 1 is estimated with low confidence to be 2 rows (86 bytes).
   The estimated time for this step is 0.03 seconds.
4) Finally, we send out an END TRANSACTION step to all AMPs involved
   in processing the request.
-> The contents of Spool 1 are sent back to the user as the result of
   statement 1.  The total estimated time is 0.03 seconds.
```

Q: I thought you said that it was an English description of how Teradata was going to execute the SQL. That doesn't look like

anything my grade school English teacher would approve of. What am I suppose do with it?
A: I actually did say "English like". Initially, we are just introducing the Explain Plan and a few of the pieces of information it contains.

Throughout the rest of the book we will periodically use explain plans to validate examples. The Explain plan is one of the most useful tools available for understanding Teradata concepts. Introducing the EXPLAIN command now provides the opportunity to gain experience and become comfortable in reading the results produced.

Later as you developed complex SQL, the EXPLAIN plan will prove invaluable for researching poorly executing SQL statements.

Hopefully the more explain plans presented and analyzed may make them seem a little less intimidating.

Q: The first thing that I like is that it gives me an estimate of how long the query is going to take to execute. That is pretty cool isn't it?
A: As long as you understand that it is an estimate. While in some cases it may be close to the actual execution time, it is better to view it as a relative value.

Below are some actual estimated times that were returned in Explain plans.

```
The total estimated time is 16,788,554 hours and 5 minutes.
The total estimated time is 19,614,949,672,554 hours and 56 minutes.
The total estimated time is *** hours and -1,200,959,900,632 minutes.
```

There is a high probability that these do not correspond to an actual execution time. However, we should be able to quickly infer that the SQL associated with these time estimates has some major problems.

Q: If I understand correctly, the time estimates are valuable as a reference but they are not an exact estimation.
A: Exactly. Remember that the execution plan is created as the optimizer determines how the SQL is going to be executed. The optimizer relys on information collected in the datab in creating the execution plan and in turn the estimations. If the required information is missing or incorrect the exection plan and estimations can be greatly affected.

Even if the estimation is spot on other factors can affect the actual wall clock execution time. For example, the optimizer has no idea what the load on the system will be when the SQL is executed. A heavy load on the database server could slow execution.

Q: Wait a second. Scanning through the Explain plan it says that it estimated that the Months table has 2 rows. We inserted 12 rows into the table. Why does it think the table has 2 rows?
A: Because it doesn't know better. Look at that full sentence. The explain plan says "low confidence". That is its keyword for, I have minimal information on this metric, so I am going to try and make an educated guess.

Statistics

Q: Guessing doesn't sound very "High Tech". I would agree that the difference in thinking that a table with 2 rows, when is actually has 12, should not have much of an effect in determining an execution plan. But what about those cases where the guess is really bad?
A: Teradata provides the ability to gather statistics concerning a table that the optimizer can than access to get a better understanding of the properties involved.

The format for the SQL command is:

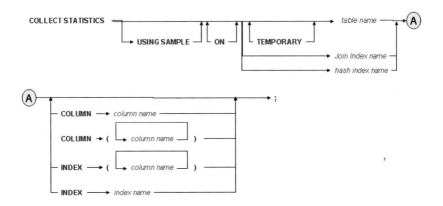

Using the syntax above, we can collect statistics on the column month_id column.

```
COLLECT STATISTICS Months COLUMN (MONTH_ID)
```

Re-running the explain plan on the simple SQL does not change the execution plan but we now can see that the explain plan show a high confidence on the number of rows to be processed.

```
EXPLAIN select * from months
1) First, we lock a distinct SYSDBA."pseudo table" for read on a
   RowHash to prevent global deadlock for SYSDBA.months.
2) Next, we lock SYSDBA.months for read.
3) We do an all-AMPs RETRIEVE step from SYSDBA.months by way of an
   all-rows scan with no residual conditions into Spool 1
   (group_amps), which is built locally on the AMPs.  The size of
   Spool 1 is estimated with high confidence to be 12 rows (516
   bytes).  The estimated time for this step is 0.03 seconds.
4) Finally, we send out an END TRANSACTION step to all AMPs involved
   in processing the request.
-> The contents of Spool 1 are sent back to the user as the result of
   statement 1.  The total estimated time is 0.03 seconds.
```

Q: So how do know what columns or indexes I need to collect statistics on.

A: That can be an issue. Basically you should collect statistics on all indexes and columns that participate in a join condition.

Here is an example of the importance of collecting statistics. We first create a simple table as shown:

```
CREATE SET TABLE IndexTable        (
     Table_id    INTEGER,
     Name        CHAR(256) )
PRIMARY INDEX ( Table_id )
INDEX ( Name );
```

The table contains two columns. The first column is an integer value to be used for identification. The second column is a character name field. On this table we create a secondary index on the name column. I understand we have not discussed Secondary Indexes are yet, but at this point we are just illustrating the importance of statistics. We will discuss Secondary Indexes in excruciating detail later.

The table is then inserted with 7000 rows of dummy data. Executing a SQL that contains a where clause referencing the name column results in the following execution plan.

```
EXPLAIN select name from indextable where name = 'abc'
  1) First, we lock a distinct sysDBA."pseudo table" for read on a
                        •
  3) We do an all-AMPs RETRIEVE step from sysDBA..indextable by way of
     an all-rows scan with a condition of ("sysDBA.indextable.Name =
     'abc'") into Spool 1 (group_amps), which is built locally on the
     AMPs.  The size of Spool 1 is estimated with no confidence to be
     677 rows.  The estimated time for this step is 0.01 seconds.
```

Reading the Explain Plan determines that we are doing a full table scan to retrieve the rows that meet the where clause condition.

After statistics are collect on the secondary index, the same SQL now shows a different execution plan.

```
EXPLAIN select name from indextable where name = 'abc'
  1) First, we lock a distinct sysDBA."pseudo table" for read on a
                        •

  3) We do an all-AMPs RETRIEVE step from sysDBA.indextable by way of
     index # 4 " sysDBA.indextable.Name = 'abc'" with no residual
     conditions into Spool 1 (group_amps), which is built locally on
     the AMPs.  The size of Spool 1 is estimated with high confidence
     to be 1 row.  The estimated time for this step is 0.01 seconds.
                        •

                        •
```

Teradata only decides to use the secondary index we created when statistics have been collected on that index.

Q: Reviewing the syntax for the Collect Statistics statement, I see that I can execute the statement with out listing any columns or indexes. Does that mean if the Collect Statistics statement only lists a table name, Teradata automatically determines what statistics need to be collected?
A: You wish. If you issue a collect statistics statement with only a table name, the statistics that already exist are refreshed.

Q: Wait a minute, you mean I have to refresh the statistics?
A: Yes, it is very important to have up to date statistics. Old statistics that to not reflect the correct state of a table can many times be worse than no statistics at all.

Q: How do I know what statistics exist on a table?
A: The Help Statistics statement will display the statistics that are currently defined on a table.

```
HELP STATISTICS Months
Date                  Time         Unique Values  Column Names
13/12/17              12:14:20     12             Month_Id
```

Q: Oh come on, there must be something available to at least give me a starting point in figuring out what to collect statistics on?
A: Well there is a secret option that can help provide some initial guidance for collecting statistics.

There exists a diagnostic command that can turn on a helpstats feature. With this feature enabled, creating an explain plan for a SQL that will access the tables in question, will include an additional final step. This step will detail collect statistics commands that the optimizer would have liked to have been collected.

Here in this example, helpstats is enabled and then we execute an EXPLAIN for a SQL query that joins two tables.

```
diagnostic helpstats on for session;
explain select * from potus p, state s where p.state_born_id = s.state_id;
  1) First, we lock a distinct SYSDBA."pseudo table" for read on a
     RowHash to prevent global deadlock for SYSDBA.s.
     • • •
  6) Finally, we send out an END TRANSACTION step to all AMPs involved
     in processing the request.
  -> The contents of Spool 1 are sent back to the user as the result of
     statement 1.  The total estimated time is 0.06 seconds.
     BEGIN RECOMMENDED STATS ->
  7) "COLLECT STATISTICS SYSDBA.potus COLUMN STATE_BORN_ID".
     (HighConf)
     <- END RECOMMENDED STATS
```

At the end of the explain plan, Teradata has included a Step 7 that suggests collecting statistics on the STATE_BORN_ID column, Teradata believes having these statistics is important in generating the most optimal execution plan.

The recommendations produced by helpstats are not an absolute but can assist as a starting point is determining what statistics are going to be required.

The command above enables helpstats for your current session. To disable helpstats you can execute:

```
diagnostic helpstats off for session;
```

Table Properties

Q: Is there any way in Teradata that I can query information about an existing table?
A: Of course. Teradata provides two commands that can assist you in extracting information about an existing table. The SHOW command returns a creation SQL for the object specified. We can execute the SHOW command specifying a table to see the details of how a table was defined.

If we execute the following SQL, the resulting answerset will display the creation SQL for the table:

```
show table months;
CREATE SET TABLE SYSDBA.months ,NO FALLBACK ,
     NO BEFORE JOURNAL,
     NO AFTER JOURNAL,
     CHECKSUM = DEFAULT
     (
      Month_Id INTEGER,
      Description VARCHAR(50) CHARACTER SET LATIN NOT CASESPECIFIC)
PRIMARY INDEX ( Month_Id );
```

Q: I can see where the show command can be very useful. Not only would be helpful to see the details of an existing table but I could use it to generate a template SQL if I needed to create a table with a similar structure. So what is the other option available for getting table information?
A: The HELP command can be used to see detailed information about the columns in a table.

Executing the HELP command returns a separate row for each column in the table.

```
help table months;
```

Column Name	Type	Comment	Nullable	Format	Title	Max Length	Decimal Total Digits	Decimal Fractional Digits	Range Low	Range High	UpperCase	Table/View?	Default value	Char Type	IdCol Type
Month_Id	I		Y	--(12)9		4					N	T			
Description	CV		Y	X(50)		50					N	T			1

The HELP TABLE command is similar to the Oracle DESCR SQL Plus command.

Database and User Accounts

"Intelligence is the ability to adapt to change."

— Stephen Hawking

In this chapter we will look a little deeper at Teradata User and Database Accounts. This will include a review relating to account setup options and the SQL commands used for their creation.

Along with setting up the User and Database Account we will introduce some of the Data Dictionary views available for retrieving Database information.

In reviewing some of the additional options involved with account creation, we will get an initial exposure to some of the data protection options that are available for tables in the Teradata database.

Teradata User Accounts

Q: So, while not a supreme wizard on Teradata SQL Assistant after completing the previous section, I feel that I can at least connect to a Teradata Database and execute basic SQL commands. Where do we go from here?

A: Up until this point we have been using the SysDBA account for connecting to our training database. First, we will create an individual user account for us to utilize going forward. The Teradata SQL for creating a user with the least number of options is shown below:

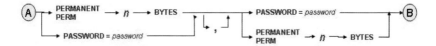

user_name: a unique name used to identify the database user we are creating.

database_name: Remember that all the accounts in Teradata are arranged in a hierarchical structure. We must specify what database or user account will be the parent. If a database_name is not specified it will default to the database for the current session.

password: a text string to be the logon password for the database user. A password must be specified. There is no default.

n: Number of bytes of permanent space the user account will be assigned. The space will be taken from unallocated permanent space assigned to the parent account. A value must be supplied. If a value of zero is specified the new user account will not be able to create objects that require perm space (i.e. tables).

Start up Teradata SQL Assistant, connect to the Teradata Demo Database and log into the database as SysSBA.

To create our first user account, execute the following SQL:

```
CREATE USER sysLIB FROM SysDBA AS PASSWORD=NewPassword PERMANENT = 0 BYTES
```

Did the account get created correctly?

Q: No. I think I was set up. I got the following error:

```
CREATE USER sysLIB FROM SysDBA AS PASSWORD=NewPassword PERMANENT = 0 BYTES
A user, database or role with the specified name already exists.
```

I guess when you wanted me to create a new user; I just assumed we were going to "successfully" create a user. How, do I know what names are in use?
A: I was just testing to make sure you actually read about the restrictions on the user_name above.

One way to check to see if a username has already been defined for an object is to query Teradata's Data Dictionary.

Teradata's Data Dictionary contains all the information Teradata needs to function correctly. This includes information on all objects defined in the database such as; users, databases, tables, views and roles.

The final chapter will be dedicated to an in-depth discussion of Teradata's Data Dictionary. However, a quick exposure to some of the information contained in the Data Dictionary will be valuable at this point.

A potential user account name can not already exist in the database for another user, database or role. To verify that a proposed name does not exist in the database, we can query the Data Dictionary Views to determine if it already exists.

The following Data Dictionary views can provide this information:

Data Dictionary View	Description
DBC.Users	Contains information about users defined in the database.
DBC.Databases	Contains information about databases defined in the database.
DBC.RoleInfo	Contains information about Roles defined in the system

Go ahead and do a SELECT * FROM DBC.xxxxxx for each of these tables.

Q: There appears to be a lot of interesting information detailed in these Data Dictionary Views. However, I notice there are names that are the same in the DBC.Users view and in the DBC.Databases view. I thought that we couldn't duplicate names.
A: That is true. If you look closer you will see a column in the DBC.Databases view called DBKind. The DBC.Databases view details all accounts and has an

indicator column, DBKind to differentiate between the two types. We will look at this in more detail in the Data Dictionary chapter.

To accomplish our goal for identifying names already in use we can just look at the DBC.Databases view and the DBC.RoleInfo view. A sample SQL to accomplish this is:

```
SELECT
      (CASE WHEN DBKind = 'U' THEN 'User' ELSE 'Database' END) "Object",
      DatabaseName "Name"
FROM
      dbc.Databases
UNION
SELECT
      'Role'    "Object",
      RoleName "Name"
FROM
      DBC.RoleInfo
ORDER BY
      2;
Object       Name
User         All
User         Crashdumps
User         DBC
User         Default
User         EXTUSER

....... Partial Display of Returned Rows
```

Execute this SQL and review the results.

Go back to our original CREATE USER sql and create an account. This time, assign 10 mBytes of PERM space to your user account.

```
CREATE USER myName FROM SysDBA AS PASSWORD=XYZZY PERMANENT = 10485760
BYTES
```

Q: Now what is the problem? I believe I executed the CREATE USER command exactly as you specified but still got an error message.

```
CREATE USER myName FROM SysDBA AS PASSWORD=XYZZY PERMANENT = 10485760
BYTES
The request to assign new PERMANENT space is invalid.
```

The syntax looks correct. What else am I forgetting?
A: Remember from our previous discussions that all Permanent Space has to come from somewhere. When you create a User Account and give it PERM Space that amount of space is taken from the parent account. In this case, SysDBA does not have 10 Mbytes of space to give the new User account you are creating.

You can query the DBC.DiskSpace Data Dictionary view to determine how much Perm Space a user or account has assigned. The SQL statement below will display the amount of space that has been assigned to sysDBA.

```
select
      sum(MaxPerm) / 1024 / 1024 as TotalSpace
from
      dbc.diskspace
where
```

```
          databasename='SysDBA'
TotalSpace
20
```

Q: OK, but as is indicated in the result returned by your SQL, sysDBA appears to have 20 Mbytes assigned. I was only trying to assign myName 10 Mbytes. I do not understand why the CREATE USER failed.

A: You are correct that sysDBA has a maximum PERM Space allocation of 20 Mbytes; however you also need to check if SysDBA has allocated any of this space to other objects. Summing the column CurrentPerm will return the amount of space that sysDBA is currently using. Subtracting this from the sum of MaxPerm will reviel how much space is still available.

```
SELECT
        (sum(MaxPerm)  - sum(CurrentPerm)) / 1024 / 1024 Available
FROM
        dbc.diskspace
WHERE
        databasename='SysDBA'
Available
5.45703125
```

We can see that sysDBA has a little over 5 Mbytes available. If we try to execute the CREATE USER command assigning 1 Mbyte of PERM Space to the account, it should not succeed.

```
CREATE USER myName FROM SysDBA AS PASSWORD=XYZZY PERMANENT = 1048576 BYTES
```

After the CREATE USER statement completes successfully, we should be able to connect to the database as the newly defined user.

Q: Eureka! It worked! I was even able to connect to the database using the new account. I have another question concerning space management. What do you do if a new user needs more space than what is allocated to its parent?

A: We need to use the GIVE SQL statement. The GIVE statement switches the ownership (parent) of a user or database account to a different user or database account. The syntax for the GIVE statement is:

The other concept you need to know is what happens to a user or database space when the account is dropped. When a user or database account is dropped the PERM space that was assigned to it is returned to its owner (parent). Using these two items together allows us transfer space from any account to another account.

Consider the following set of SQL:

`CREATE DATABASE "TTBtempDB" FROM` `"AccountWithSpace" AS PERM = n BYTES;`	First we create a temporary database, where the parent has the space we want to transfer.
`GIVE "TTBtempDB" TO` `"AccountThatNeedsSpace";`	Using the GIVE statement we transfer ownership of the account, including the PERM space, to the account that needs the space.
`DROP DATABASE "TTBtempDB";`	Now when we drop the temporary database, the space that was allocated to it is returned to its parent. This is where we needed the space.

Q: That sure seems a roundabout way to move storage around but the procedure makes sense. By the way, what is with the CREATE DATABASE command? We haven't discussed that yet, have we?
A: Sorry for jumping the gun. The CREATE DATABASE SQL command creates a new database account. A database account is very similar to a user account except that you can not log into a database account. They only hold objects. The simplest command syntax for creating a database is:

To give a specific example of creating database accounts and moving space around between them we will create the TRAIN_1 and TRAIN_2 databases. Both databases will be children of sysDBA.

TRAIN_1 will initially be assigned 2 K of PERM SPACE.

```
CREATE DATABASE TRAIN_1 FROM SysDBA AS PERM = 2048 BYTES;
```

TRAIN_2 will be created with an initial PERM SPACE assignment of 1 K.

```
CREATE DATABASE TRAIN_2 FROM SysDBA AS PERM = 1024 BYTES;
```

Using the previous SQL command , we can validate that the new accounts were created with the desired PERM SPACE allocations.

```
select
      databasename,
      sum(MaxPerm) as PERMspace
from
      dbc.diskspace
where
      databasename in ('TRAIN_1', 'TRAIN_2')
group by 1
```

DatabaseName	PERMspace
TRAIN_1	2048
TRAIN_2	1024

Now suppose we need to move 1K of PERM SPACE that is assigned to TRAIN_1
to TRAIN_2.

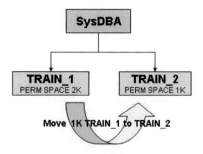

**Q: Based on the procedure you presented, I believe the first step
would be to create a temporary database as a child of TRAIN_1
giving it a PERM SPACE allocation of 1 K. Correct?**
A: Exactly. The first step in moving the space would be to create a temporary
database account and allocate it the 1K.

```
CREATE DATABASE TTBtempDB FROM TRAIN_1 AS PERM = 1024 BYTES;
```

Once the temporary database has been created we can use the GIVE command
to transfer ownership of the database from TRAIN_1 to TRAIN_2

```
GIVE TTBtempDB to TRAIN_2;
```

Finally, when we drop the temporary database, the space allocated to the
database is returned to it's parent. Since the parent of the temporary database
is now TRAIN_2, TRAIN_2 will now get the 1 K PERM SPACE allocation.

```
DROP   DATABASE TTBtempDB;
```

Now when we display the PERM SPACE allocations for the two databases, we
can see that 1 K has been successfully transferred.

```
select
      databasename,
      sum(MaxPerm) as PERMspace
from
      dbc.diskspace
where
      databasename in ('TRAIN_1', 'TRAIN_2')
group by 1
DatabaseName   PERMspace
TRAIN_1        1024
TRAIN_2        2048
```

**Q: How about a few words about the other SQL that you referenced
but have failed to go into details yet, the DROP DATABASE?**
A: It is encouraging to hear that you are interested in keeping things clean and
tidy.

The DROP DATABASE and DROP USER command is used to remove databases from the system. The format of the commands is:

DROP USER ⟶ user_name ⟶ ;

DROP DATABASE ⟶ database_name ⟶ ;

To demonstrate a feature of the DROP command lets first create a table object in our TRAIN_2 database.

```
create table train_2.simple (simple_id integer);
```

Now drop the TRAIN_1 and TRAIN_2 databases.

```
DROP DATABASE TRAIN_1;
DROP DATABASE TRAIN_2;
```

Q: Well at least I had a hint that everything wasn't going to run perfectly this time. The drop of TRAIN_1 executed successfully but I recieved an error message when I tried to DROP TRAIN_2,

```
DROP DATABASE TRAIN_2;
Cannot DROP databases with tables, journal tables, views, or macros.
```

I don't have to call Captain Obvious to realize that the table we created was the problem. Does this mean that I have to drop all the objects a database (or user) owns before I can drop the database (or user)?
A: Dropping all of the objects is always an option; However Teradata provides a simpler way. The DELETE command will drop the user or database account and all of its contents. The format for the command is:

The ALL option is required if the user or database to be deleted contains materialized global temporary tables. With out the ALL option specified, if any materialized global temporary tables exist, the delete will fail.

Use the delete command to drop TRAIN_2.

```
DELETE DATABASE TRAIN_2;
```

Q: When we created our users and databases you mentioned that the SQL command we executed was the simplest form of the command. What options are you hiding from us?

A: Listed below are the rest of the options available when creating a user or database.

Additional Create USER / DATABASE Options	Applicable	Description
SPOOL = n BYTES	user, database	Number of bytes allowed for spool files.
TEMPORARY = n BYTES	user, database	The amount of space allowed for creating materialized global tables.
ACCOUNT = 'account_id'	user, database	Determines the account for the user.
[NO] FALLBACK [PROTECTION]	user, database	Determines whether to create a backup copy of each table created.
[NO, DUAL] BEFORE JOURNAL	user, database	Number of before images of a table to be maintained.
[NO, DUAL, LOCAL, NOT LOCAL] AFTER JOURNAL	user, database	Number of after images of a table to be maintained.
DEFAULT JOURNAL TABLE = [database_name.] table_name	user, database	Location of journal images.
DEFAULT DATABASE database_name	user	The default database the session is to be assigned. If omitted it defaults to the username
COLLATION = collation_sequence	user	Defines the Collation sequence for the session
TIMEZONE = [LOCAL, quotestring, NULL]	user	Time zone displacement for the user.
DATEFORM = [INTEGERDATE, ANSIDATE, NULL]	user	Default date format.
STARTUP = 'string'	user	Used to define a startup string to establish the session environment.
DEFAULT CHARACTER SET = server_character_set	user	User default character set
DEFAULT ROLE = [role_name, NONE, NULL, ALL]	user	The default role for the user
PROFILE = [profile_name, NULL]	user	The default profile for the user.

Q: Sorry I asked. Some of these options have been mentioned already and some of them I can guess at but a few of them seem totally new concepts. For example, what is FALLBACK?
A: For some of the options allowed in the CREATE USER and CREATE DATABASE commands, they will make more sense when we discuss that concept in detail. However now is a good time to introduce some of the more Teradata specific options?

FALLBACK protection is an optional data protection feature of Teradata. If activated, Teradata creates a copy of each row in a table on a different AMP. This way, if an AMP becomes unavailable, Teradata can still access the data from the backup copy.

The downside to FALLBACK protection is that a FALLBACK protected table requires twice the storage as a NON-FALLBACK table.

Q: That's kind of a nice feature but I would only imagine we would use FALLBACK only for super critical tables. What about the Journal options?
A: Permanent Journaling is another method for protecting your data. A permanent journal is a table where either BEFORE or AFTER images of a table's data is stored.

The Permanent Journal table can exist in the database space of the user or database account or in another account. The permanent journal does require PERMENANT SPACE. There can only be one journal file assign to a user or database account.

BEFORE journals will store an image of a row prior to it being modified. In the event of a software failure the journal can be used to roll back all transactions from a table to a checkpoint.

Similar to BEFORE journals, AFTER journals store an image of row changes but in this case the image is stored after the change has been completed. AFTER journals are used in recovery by allowing a table to be rolled forward.

Rolling back or forward is not a total automatic process. Manual intervention is required.

Q: Now I am worried. If I am running a transaction and an error occurs, does this mean that rolling back the transaction is a manual process. Since these before and after journals are optional, what happens if I do not specify journals.
A: Calm down, we have been referring to permanent journal files. To protect the integrity of data while a transaction is executing a transient journal is used. This happens without user intervention.

Any time a user executes an insert, update or delete statement, the changes are stored in the transient journal table. This table is owned by DBC and is called DBC.TransientJournal.

The data images are stored in the transient journal table to be used in case of a transaction failure or a rollback. A before image of the data is used to roll back the data to before the transaction started. This happens automatically.

Once the transactions completes, the image is deleted from the transient journal.

By querying the Data Dictionary DBC.TABLES view we can retrieve properties about the TransientJournal table. As an example if we wanted to determine if TransientJournal table is Fallback protected we could execute the SQL below:

```
SELECT
        DatabaseName,
        TableName,
        TableKind,
        ProtectionType
FROM
        dbc.tables
```

```
WHERE
      DataBaseName = 'DBC'
  and TableName = 'TransientJournal'
DatabaseName    TableName          TableKind   ProtectionType
DBC             TransientJournal   T           N
```

The view returns a ProtectionType column that contains the value 'N'. To determine what this means we need to refer to the Teradata Data Dictionary documentation. In looking this up, we can determine that the ProtectionType can have two values either a 'F' to indicate Fallback or a 'N' to indicate no protection.

ProtectionType Code Values			
F	Fallback	N	None

Additional information concerning the Teradata Data Dictionary will be covered later the Data Dictionary chapter with reference material in the appendix.

Teradata Tables

"The trouble with programmers is that you can never tell what a programmer is doing until it's too late."

— *Seymour Cray*

The core function of any database is the creation of tables to store data and the ability to manipulate that table's information.

In this section we will talk about some of the table issues that are unique to a Teradata database.

Table Creation

Q: Since Teradata is based upon ANSI standards, I would assume that the syntax for creating a table is similar to that of other databases. How much difference can there be?
A: Lets start by looking at the beginning of a syntax diagram for the create table command. You will notice the options for specifying that a table is either a SET table or a MULTISET table. In addition, a table can optionally be defined as a GLOBAL TEMPORARY or a VOLATILE table.

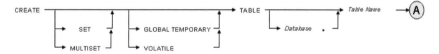

Q: I do not think that I have ever seen the SET or MULTISET option. What is the difference between the two types of table definations?
A: In simple terms a SET table can not contain any rows where the entire row's data is the same as another row. MULTISET tables are allowed to contain duplicate rows.

To show this let's first create a simple set table and try to insert two identical rows.

```
CREATE SET TABLE set_example (col1 char(1));
INSERT INTO set_example (col1) VALUES ('A');
1 Rows Inserted
INSERT INTO set_example (col1) VALUES ('A');
Duplicate row error in set_example.
```

The second insert statement fails because this would violate the duplicate row restriction of a SET table.

Now let's see what happens if we repeat the same exercise but this time we define the table as a MULTISET table.

```
CREATE MULTISET TABLE multiset_example (col1 char(1));
INSERT INTO multiset_example (col1) VALUES ('A');
1 Rows Inserted
INSERT INTO multiset_example (col1) VALUES ('A');
1 Rows Inserted
```

This time, both insert statements execute successfully.

Q: I do not want my insert statements failing; Why not just create all my tables as MULTISET tables?
A: First remember that the whole row has to be a duplicate, not just a particular columns. Also, Teradata does not provide a mechanism to address a specific row. Any SQL that you execute to return a duplicated row will always return both rows. This can easily leads to undesirable consequences. Unless the application can specifically handle duplicate rows it is not usually a desirable condition.

Defining a table as SET removes this possibility.

Q: So if defining tables as SET keeps me out of trouble, is there any reason that I would ever define a table to be MULTISET?
A: One reason is performance. When doing an INSERT, how can Teradata know if the row to be inserted is a duplicate? For a SET table, Teradata must first check to insure that the row to be inserted is unique. In a large table, this overhead can be substantial.

If a table is defined as MULTISET, this check does not have to be preformed.

Q: What about GLOBAL TEMPORARY and VOLATILE tables. How do they differ from normal tables?
A: Both are types of temporary tables, where they differ is how the table definition is stored. The definition of a GLOBAL TEMPORARY table is stored in the database data dictionary. A VOLATILE table definition is stored local to the session.

Below is an example of creating a GLOBAL TEMPORARY table. After it is created, rows can be inserted and the data manipulated like a standard table.

```
CREATE GLOBAL TEMPORARY TABLE global_example (col1 char(1));
Insert global_example (col1) values ('G');
1 Rows Inserted
```

Q: Wait a second! I ran the SQL above and it said 1 row was inserted. I then executed the query "select * from global_example" and it did not return any rows. What happened to the rows that were inserted?
A: Believe it or not it functioned exactly as it was designed. If we do a SHOW TABLE we can see the full definition of how the table was created.

```
show table global_example;
CREATE SET GLOBAL TEMPORARY TABLE global_example
     (
        col1 CHAR(1) CHARACTER SET LATIN NOT CASESPECIFIC)
PRIMARY INDEX ( col1 )
ON COMMIT DELETE ROWS;
```

Notice the last Line, ON COMMIT DELETE ROWS. This says, after a commit is executed; delete any rows that are in the table. Since our transaction was a single insert statement a commit was issued after the insert. At this point Teradata deleted the row.

While this might be useful when utilizing multiple step transactions, it is usually not what we want. The other option on the "on commit" clause is ON COMMIT PRESERVE ROWS.

In this example we have changed the "on commit" clause and we re-create our table. Now we can observe what happens.

```
CREATE GLOBAL TEMPORARY TABLE global_example (col1 char(1))
   ON COMMIT PRESERVE ROWS;
Insert global_example (col1) values ('G');
1 Rows Inserted
select * from global_example;
col1
G
```

Q: One might think that the default for the "on commit" clause is the opposite of what make sense but whatever. I am still a little confused about the difference between the VOLATILE and GLOBAL TEMPORARY tables. Can you show an example?
A: Not a problem. Let us recreate our two sample tables and then insert a row into each table.

First we will create the volatile table, insert data into the table and then verify the data has been inserted by executing a SELECT.

```
CREATE VOLATILE TABLE volatile_example (col1 char(1))
   ON COMMIT PRESERVE ROWS;
Insert volatile_example (col1) values ('V');
1 Rows Inserted
select * from volatile_example;
col1
V
```

Now we will do the same for the GLOBAL TEMPORARY table.

```
CREATE GLOBAL TEMPORARY TABLE global_example (col1 char(1))
   ON COMMIT PRESERVE ROWS;
Insert global_example (col1) values ('G');
1 Rows Inserted
select * from global_example;
col1
G
```

Q: Looking at the created tables, I can not see any difference between the tables except one is defined as VOLATILE and the other is GLOBAL TEMPORARY. I am still lost.
A: Now that the two tables have been created and populated we can demonstrate how they differ.

First we need to end our existing session and then log in to create a new connection. With the new connection, we try and select the data we inserted from each of the tables.

When we execute the SELECT statement against the VOLATILE table we
receive an error that the table doesn't exist.

```
select * from volatile_example;
Object 'volatile_example' does not exist.
```

However, when you attempt to seect the data from the global table, you see the
table exists but the data we inserted is gone.

```
select * from global_example;
col1
....... No Rows Returned
```

The table definition for a volatile table is only valid for the length of the session
that created the table. In this case when we logged out our session, the volatile
table definition was deleted.

The table definition for a global temporary table is stored in the data dictionary.
When we logged off and then reconnected, the table definition still existed.
However, the rows in the global table are associated with the session that
inserted them. When we reconnected to the database, the rows we inserted
previously were dropped when the session ended.

Primary Indexes

**Q: I thought that we had already talked about Primary Indexes.
They determine how the rows are distributed across the AMP
thingies. What else is there?**
A: The primary index is probably the most important concept in Teradata.
Determining what the primary key will be for a table is critical in determining
the ultimate performance for accessing the table. The primary key determines
where the data for a row is stored which directly determines how the data will
need to be accessed.

The Primary Index can be defined as a Unique Primary Index (UPI) where the
values of the index do not contain any duplicates. Alternately, if the Primary
Index is required to have duplicate values it can be created as a Non-Unique
Primary Index (NUPI).

Unique Primary Index (UPI)

**Q: I cannot believe it is that important. Are you sure it is not one of
those things that Teradata says just to make it seem mystical?**
A: Not at all. In fact, if you understand the concept of the Primary Index and
how it is utilized, all the Teradata magic suddenly becomes unveiled.

First, a few things about primary indexes. As we mentioned before, all tables in
Teradata have a Primary Index. The Primary Index can be comprised of a

single column or multiple columns. The entire Primary Index is used to determine which AMP the row is going to be located on.

Let's look at a simple example. Here we create a very simple table comprised of three columns of data. The first column is defined as a unique primary index.

```
CREATE SET TABLE PIsample
       (Col_1 CHAR(1)
       ,Col_2 CHAR(1)
       ,Col_3 CHAR(1) )
UNIQUE PRIMARY INDEX (Col_1);
```

Now we execute a select SQL that retrieves data based on the Primary Index.

```
select col_3 from PIsample where Col_1='A'
```

If we do an EXPLAIN plan of this SQL we can determine how Teradata is going to retrieve the data. We know that the Primary Key is unique and thus one a single row will be returned. Also, we know that the value of Col_1 will determine the AMP where the row is located. To retrieve the row, we just need to determine the AMP that is storing the 'A' values and then set a single request to that AMP to retrieve the row.

```
EXPLAIN select col_3 from PIsample where Col_1='A'
   1) First, we do a single-AMP RETRIEVE step from sysDBA.PIsample by
      way of the unique primary index "sysDBA.PIsample.Col_1 = 'A'"
      with no residual conditions.  The estimated time for this step is
      0.01 seconds.
  -> The row is sent directly back to the user as the result of
      statement 1.  The total estimated time is 0.01 seconds.
```

When reading the explain plan a key phrase is "single-AMP RETRIEVE". This indicates a highly efficient operation where only 1 AMP will be involved to the retrieval.

Non-Unique Primary Index (NUPI)

Q: Why would it make a difference if the Primary Key was unique? While we wouldn't know if more than one row existed, all the rows would still be on the same AMP. Doesn't Teradata handle the execution the same?
A: Good observation that the rows would exist on the same AMP. That is an important point to comprehend. To answer your question, let's actually re-create the table with a non-unique Primary Index.

```
CREATE SET TABLE PIsample
       (Col_1 CHAR(1)
       ,Col_2 CHAR(1)
       ,Col_3 CHAR(1) )
PRIMARY INDEX (Col_1);
```

Using the same SQL as before, we now review the execution plan that is generated.

```
EXPLAIN select col_3 from PIsample where Col_1='A'
```

```
1) First, we do a single-AMP RETRIEVE step from sysDBA.PIsample by
   way of the primary index " sysDBA.PIsample.Col_1 = 'A'" with no
   residual conditions into Spool 1 (one-amp), which is built locally
   on that AMP.  The size of Spool 1 is estimated with low confidence
   to be 2 rows.  The estimated time for this step is 0.01 seconds.
-> The contents of Spool 1 are sent back to the user as the result of
   statement 1.  The total estimated time is 0.01 seconds.
```

By studying the explain plan we can determine that Teradata indeed utilizes a single AMP in retrieving the rows. However, notice that the result set is first stored in a Spool table. The rows in Spool table are then returned to the user as the result set.

Q: Interesting, so having a non-unique primary index is still an efficient construct. However it is just not as efficient as using a unique primary index. Would it be a good idea then to make my primary index unique by defining it with multiple columns to make it unique?
A: That is dependent on how you are going to access the data. If we go back to our sample table and re-create it again but now with a Primary Index comprised of both col_1 and col_2.

```
CREATE SET TABLE PIsample
      (Col_1 CHAR(1)
      ,Col_2 CHAR(1)
      ,Col_3 CHAR(1) )
UNIQUE PRIMARY INDEX (Col_1, Col_2)
```

If we execute a select SQL with a where clause containing both col_1 and col_2 we get our efficient 1-AMP execution plan.

```
EXPLAIN select col_3 from PIsample where Col_1='A' and Col_2='B'
  1) First, we do a single-AMP RETRIEVE step from sysDBA.PIsample by
     way of the unique primary index " sysDBA.PIsample.Col_1 = 'A',
     sysDBA.PIsample.Col_2 = 'B'" with no residual conditions.  The
     estimated time for this step is 0.01 seconds.
  -> The row is sent directly back to the user as the result of
     statement 1.  The total estimated time is 0.01 seconds.
```

However, if we executed our original SQL where the where clause only contained a reference to col_1 we get the following execution plan.

```
EXPLAIN select col_3 from PIsample where Col_1='A'
  1) First, we lock a distinct sysDBA."pseudo table" for read on a
     RowHash to prevent global deadlock for sysDBA.PIsample.
  2) Next, we lock sysDBA.PIsample for read.
  3) We do an all-AMPs RETRIEVE step from sysDBA.PIsample by way of
     an all-rows scan with a condition of ("sysDBA.PIsample.Col_1 =
     'A'") into Spool 1 (group_amps), which is built locally on the
     AMPs.  The size of Spool 1 is estimated with no confidence to be 1
     row.  The estimated time for this step is 0.03 seconds.
  4) Finally, we send out an END TRANSACTION step to all AMPs involved
     in processing the request.
  -> The contents of Spool 1 are sent back to the user as the result of
     statement 1.  The total estimated time is 0.03 seconds.
```

Look at step 3. The phrase "all-AMPs RETRIEVE" indicates that Teradata will instruct all AMPs to search for the result rows. We now have a full table scan.

Q: Wait. Why does Teradata have to do a full table scan? Why can it not use the Primary Index to at least par down the number of rows that need to be looked at?
A: Remember, all columns that are part of the Primary Index are used to determine which AMP the row will reside on. Since the Primary Index was col_1 and col_2, both values were utilized in this determination. There is no guarantee that that is the same AMP as col_1 by itself. Thus, the only way Teradata can find all the rows where col_1 is equal to an 'A' is to search the entire table. The Primary Index is of no value in the search.

Data Distribution

Q: So in Teradata, like most other databases, the goal is to avoid full table scans at all costs.
A: Not necessarily. While it is always nice if we can access a row with a single operation on a single AMP, one of the powers of Teradata comes from doing tasks in parallel. A full table scan can be less painful if we are able to divide the work across all the available AMPs. This allows each AMP to perform a portion of the task.

The Primary Index is the key as to how data and thus the work is divided up. The rows of a table are divided up across all the available AMPs based on the Primary Index. A HASH function is applied to the value of the columns that make up the Primary Index and that is used to determine which AMP a row will reside.

The key is to pick a Primary Index whose values will spread the rows across the AMPs as evenly as possible.

Q: How does this HASH function work?
A: Given a data value, the HASH function returns a random hash value. The output from the Teradata hashing function is refered to as the "Row HASH". The HASH value returned will always be the same given the same data and data type.

A HASH Map is comprised of HASH buckets that contain the AMP assign for each HASH value. Using the HASH Map and the HASH value, the AMP that is going to hold the row can be determined.

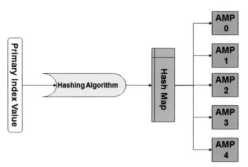

To be able to fully take advantage of the power of Teradata, we need the data to spread evenly across the AMPs.

Q: Do I have any control over the Hashing algorithm? How do I make sure my table is distributed equally?
A: Teradata has a single hashing algorithm used in the creation of Primary Indexes. Since the same value will always generate the same HASH value, having a lot of duplicate Primary Index values could skew the number of rows that are on a specific AMP. A small number of unique values will also cause a poor AMP distribution.

Teradata provides some functions that can be utilized to assist with determining how well a list of values will perform.

The function **HASHROW()** will return the HASH Value for a given data value.

The function **HASHBUCKET()** will take a HASH Value and return the Hash Bucket .

Given the Hash Bucket value, the Function **HASHAMP** () will return the AMP where that data will reside.

So, if we cascade these functions together we can write a SQL statement that will return the AMP where a row will reside for a given data value.

```
select HASHAMP(HASHBUCKET(HASHROW('ABCDEF'))) "AMP";
AMP
1
```

In the example above, if the value for a Primary Index was "ABCDEF", on this database, the row would be placed on AMP 1.

Q: Interesting piece of information but if Teradata takes care of all the hashing and distribution, why is it important to me?
A: Well, we have already talked about how important it is for the data to be equally spread across all the AMPS. Using the functions above we can determine if a Primary Index is providing a good distribution or if a different Primary Index would be better.

The employee table resides on a 2 AMP Teradata database. The following SQL will show us the distribution of the table based on the current Primary Index.

```
select
      HASHAMP(HASHBUCKET(HASHROW(empno))) "AMP",
      count(*) "Rows"
from
      employee
group by 1;
```

AMP	Rows
0	499
1	501

From the results, we can observe a nearly perfect distribution based on the column "empno".

If we were wondering what the distribution would look like if a different column was used as the Primary Index, substituting the column names would provide the answer.

```
select
      HASHAMP(HASHBUCKET(HASHROW(MedStat))) "AMP",
      count(*) "Rows"
from
      retail.employee
group by 1;
```

AMP	Rows
0	795
1	205

The AMP distribution based on the column "MedStat" is significantly poorer than when using the column "empno".

Rows, Columns and Limitations.

Q: Rows are stored on the AMPs based on the Primary Index, this makes sense now. It also makes sense that a good distribution across the AMPs is important for storage utilization and performance. What about how the rows are stored on the AMPs itself? Is there anything important to understand?
A: A couple of things. Rows are grouped together and stored in a "Data Block". While the maximum data block has grown over evolving versions of Teradata, it is a fixed value. A key piece of information is that a row cannot span a data block.

In this example, we will try and create a table with a very large row size.

```
create table BigRow (
      r1 varchar(16000),
      r2 varchar(16000),
      r3 varchar(16000),
      r4 varchar(16000),
      r5 varchar(232)
);
The Maximum Possible Row Length in the Table is too Large.
```

When our r5 column was defined to have a maximium length of 231, the
CREATE TABLE command succeeded. For this environment, we are only able
to create a table where the maximum row length will be less than 64,232 bytes
in length.

**Q: While I agree that a having a maximum row length of
approximately 64K is small, how does this effect performance?**
A: When scanning a table, the smallest unit retrieved is the data block. Multiple
rows can be stored in a single data block as long as it doesn't exceed the
maximum size restriction. Having smaller rows means more rows are retrieved
with a single read. Thus, the more rows we pack into a single data block the
better the performance.

**Q: What about the number of columns? Is there a limit to the
number of columns a table can have?**
A: We could read the manual, but what fun would that be. Like we did with the
maximum row size, we will keep creating a table adding another column to it
every time. When it fails we should have our answer.

```
CREATE SET TABLE ColTest
    (
    pi INTEGER,
    col1 CHAR(1) ,
    col2 CHAR(1) ,
    col3 CHAR(1) ,
    col4 CHAR(1) ,
         .
         .
         .
    col2044 CHAR(1) ,
    col2045 CHAR(1) ,
    col2046 CHAR(1) ,
    col2047 CHAR(1) ,
    col2048 CHAR(1) )
PRIMARY INDEX ( pi ),
Table has too many columns.
```

From our little test we can deduce that a Teradata table can have a maximum of
2048 columns. Probably large enough for most applications but still a
limitation that should be kept in mind.

Data Types

**Q: Now that we have reviewed the Teradata specifics relating to
table types and the whole Primary Index concept, what about
column definitions? Are the data types for the columns the same?**
A: They are similar to your other favorite database. Below is listed some of the
common Teradata data types and some of their properties.

Starting with the numeric datatypes:

Numeric Data Types

Data Type	Value Range	Size
Decimal	1 to 2 digits	1 byte
	3 to 4 digits	2 bytes
	5 to 9 digits	4 bytes
	10 to 18 digits	8 bytes
Byteint	-128 to +127	1 byte
Smallint	-32,768 to +32,767	2 bytes
Integer	-2,147,483,648 to +2,147,483,647	4 bytes
Float	$2*10^{-307}$ to $2*10^{+308}$	8 bytes

For character data types the primary types are char and varchar

Character Data Types

Data Type	Size Range
Character	1 - 64,000
Varchar	1 - 64,000
Long Varchar	64,000
Clob	1 to 2 gBytes

There are 5 different date and time data types to choose from.

Date and Time Data Types

Data Type	Size
Date	4 bytes
Time	6 bytes
Time with Time Zone	8 bytes
Timestamp	10 bytes
Timestamp with Time Zone	12 bytes

Q: It appears that Teradata supports all the normal data types usually available. Interesting that so many of the data types have different sizes available. Do you have any guesses as to why?
A: Remember the examples we just looked at. We have determined that with the row size limitations and the fact that the more rows we can get into a data block the better the performance, the smaller we can make our row length the better off we will be.

When creating a column definition, having multiple data types with varrying lengths can be valuable in creating an efficient table design.

Q: I didn't really make the correlation initially but now it makes sense. How do I go about converting from one data type to anouther? Does Teradata support functions like TO_CHAR and TO_NUMBER.
A: TO_CHAR and TO_NUMBER are Oracle specific conversion functions. In Teradata you need to utilize the CAST function to convert between data types.

The syntax for the CAST statement is:

For an example, if we needed to convert the string '1234' into an integer you could use the following SQL call.

```
select cast('1234' as integer) as CastExample
CastExample
1234
```

To the reverse process and convert an integer to a string, we could use:

```
select cast(1234 as char(4)) as CastExample
CastExample
1234
```

Q: When converting something to a string, what happens if the string is defined too small?
A: The simplest way to answer your question is to give it a try and see what happens.

```
select cast(1234 as char(2)) as CastExample
CastExample
12
```

As can be seen from our test, the result string is truncated to the the length specified in the data type definition of the CAST function.
Q: So how does the format option work with the CAST function?
A: The format option in the CAST function allows us to format the the value according to the format mask specified.

Formatting a numeric value to display as a currency string, the following format mask can be used.

```
select cast(1234.56 as format '$9,999.99' ) as CastExample;
CastExample
$1,234.56
```

Q: I executed what you specified above and did not get the same result you did. What happened?

```
select cast(1234.56 as format '$9,999.99' ) as CastExample;
CastExample
1,234.56
```

A: Based on your results, I am assuming that you executed your SQL in "Teradata SQL Assistant". The issue is that "Teradata SQL Assistant" connects to Teradata via an ODBC driver. My example was executed in BTEQ which connects directly to Teradata.

The FORMAT option does not change the data type. So while we told Teradata to format the number according to the FORMAT MASK we provided it was still a numeric data type. ODBC formatted the numeric value according to its default formatting.

To display the value formatting in "Teradata SQL Assistant" we need to change the data type as well as applying a format. To accomplish this we need to use two CAST functions.

```
select cast(cast(1234.56 as format '$9,999.99' ) as varchar(25)) as
CastExample;
CastExample
$1,234.56
```

Q: Weird but "it is what it is". What formatting codes are available?
A: There are different formatting codes available for character data and numeric data. For character data there is basically one formatting code.

Character String Format Codes	
X or X(n)	Each X indicates a character. Characters processed left to right.

Q: Sorry but that looks fairly useless. What is available for formatting numeric values?
A: In many ways that is true. For formatting strings many times it is easier to use a CAST function to truncate or pad the string. In addition, built-in string functions along with concatenation operators provide a flexiable option.

The chart below llists the available formatting codes for numeric data types. If you are formatting the numeric values to display as a monetary amount, there are a couple of extra codes available.

Numeric Format Codes			
Character Code	Description	Numeric	Currency
G	Indicates Currency Grouping Rule	√	√
D	Radix symbol	√	√
/ or : or %	Character copied to Output String	√	√
,	Comma	√	√
.	Currency Radix Symbol	√	√
B	Blank Character	√	√
+ or -	Positive / Negative Character	√	√
V	Implied Decimal Position	√	√
Z or Z(n)	Zero-Supressed Decimal Digit	√	√
9 or 9(n)	Decimal Digit	√	√
E	Exponential Notation	√	√
-	Dash Character	√	√
S	Signed Zoned Decimal	√	√
$ or £ or ¥ or €	Currency Sign		√
L,C,N,O,U,A	Currency Characters		√

Q: How about an example?
A: The format CAST example above demonstrates formatting a numeric value into a currency string.

Below we format a numeric value into a standard telephone string format.

```
select cast('>' ||
            cast(7732832499 as format 'B999-999-9999B') ||
          '<' as varchar(25)) as CastExample;
CastExample
> 773-283-2499 <
```

Q: What about date and time values?

A: Later we will dedicate an entire chapter to discussing Teradata date, time and timestamp data types.

Hold on just a little bit and hopefully we will answer the rest of your formatting questions.

Additional Table Topics

"The hardest thing is to go to sleep at night, when there are so many urgent things needing to be done. A huge gap exists between what we know is possible with today's machines and what we have so far been able to finish."

— *Donald Knuth*

Join Processing

Q: In all of our discussions so far we have looked at single tables and simple SELECT statements. How does Teradata handle joining tables when the tables are broken up and spread over multiple AMPs?
A: That is an important topic that is critical in understanding how Teradata handles retrieving data from the database.

To help illustrate the point, lets create a couple of simple tables. Initially we will create a POTUS table and a POTUS_YEAR table as shown below and populate the tables with a few values.

```
CREATE TABLE potus
     (
     potus_id        INTEGER,
     state_born_id INTEGER,
     name            VARCHAR(256) )
PRIMARY INDEX ( potus_id );


INSERT INTO potus   Values (1,810,'George Washington');
INSERT INTO potus   Values (2,802,'John Adams');
INSERT INTO potus   Values (3,810,'Thomas Jefferson');
INSERT INTO potus   Values (4,810,'James Madison');
INSERT INTO potus   Values (5,810,'James Monroe');
INSERT INTO potus   Values (6,802,'John Quincy Adams');
INSERT INTO potus   Values (7,830,'Andrew Jackson');

create table potus_year
     (
     potus_id        INTEGER,
     YearElectted INTEGER )
PRIMARY INDEX ( potus_id );

INSERT INTO potus_year values (1,  1732);
INSERT INTO potus_year values (2,  1735);
INSERT INTO potus_year values (3,  1743);
INSERT INTO potus_year values (4,  1751);
INSERT INTO potus_year values (5,  1758);
INSERT INTO potus_year values (6,  1765);
INSERT INTO potus_year values (7,  1767);
```

Now we execute a SELECT statement where we join the two tables on the primary index column. Note that the potus_id column is the primary index for both tables. Since the value in either of the potus_id columns will result in the same hash value, we know that the two tables will be distributed across the available AMPS the same.

```
select * from potus p, potus_year y where p.potus_id = y.potus_id
```

As detailed in the diagram showing a single AMP below, all of the data that is needed to build the result set rows is located on the same AMP. Each AMP will build the portion of the result set in parallel locally and then all the AMPs will return the final consolidated result set.

		AMP 1		
POTUS Table				
POTUS_ID	STATE_BORN_ID	NAME		
2	802	John Adams		
4	810	James Madison		
7	830	Andrew Jackson		

POTUS_YEAR Table	
POTUS_ID	YEAR_ELECTED
2	1735
4	1743
7	1767

		Result SPOOL Table		
POTUS_ID	STATE_BORN_ID	NAME	POTUS_ID	YEAR_ELECTED
2	802	John Adams	2	1735
4	810	James Madison	4	1743
7	830	Andrew Jackson	7	1767

Looking at a portion of the explain plan that was generated for the query we can see that the rows from the two tables are joined together using a all-AMP join. The explain plan validates the process discussed by indicating the result is "built locally".

```
4) We do an all-AMPs JOIN step from SYSDBA.y by way of a RowHash
   match scan, which is joined to SYSDBA.p by way of a RowHash match
   scan.  SYSDBA.y and SYSDBA.p are joined using a merge join, with a
   join condition of ("SYSDBA.p.potus_id = SYSDBA.y.potus_id").  The
   result goes into Spool 1 (group_amps), which is built locally on
   the AMPs.  The size of Spool 1 is estimated with low confidence to
   be 2 rows (248 bytes).  The estimated time for this step is 0.04
   seconds.
```

This provides us with an efficient parallel join operation. This is possible only because both tables utilize the same primary index.

Q: I understand in the example you presented how Teradata could easily perform the join but the design is terrible. To me it would be a rare occurrence that two tables would be joined in such a manor. How can we join two tables when the data is distributed differently?
A: You are right. To join tables where the data is distributed differently we need to perform some work before we are able to actually join the data.

To expand our example, we will create another table STATE. The primary index for the STATE table is the STATE_ID column.

```
create table state (
      state_id      INTEGER,
      state_name    VARCHAR(256),
      state_capital VARCHAR(256) )
UNIQUE PRIMARY INDEX ( state_id );

INSERT INTO state  Values (802,'Massachusetts', 'Boston');
INSERT INTO state  Values (830,'Tennessee', 'Nashville');
INSERT INTO state  Values (810,'Virginia', 'Richmond');
```

If we now try to join the POTUS table to the STATE table we run into the problem that the individual AMPs do not have all the data they need locally to perform the join.

```
select * from potus p, state s where p.state_born_id = s.state_id
```

Remember that AMPs cannot share anything. So to resolve this issue we will need to reorganize the data so that the AMPs have the data they need to perform the join.

One way Teradata accomplishes this is to redistribute one of the tables so that the data is distributed the same way as the other table. In our example, we can temporarily create a copy of the POTUS table where the primary index is the STATE_BORN_ID column.

Once the POTUS table is redistributed the individual AMPs have all the data they require locally to complete the join to the STATE table.

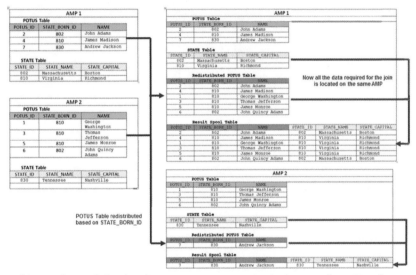

POTUS Table redistributed based on STATE_BORN_ID

Looking at the explain plan for our query we can see in Step 4 where Teradata redistributed the POTUS table based on the STATE_BORN_ID column into the SPOOL 2 table.

Then in Step 5 the STATE table is joined to Spool 2 locally on each AMP in parallel.

```
4) We do an all-AMPs RETRIEVE step from SYSDBA.p by way of an
   all-rows scan with a condition of ("NOT (SYSDBA.p.state_born_id IS
   NULL)") into Spool 2 (all_amps), which is redistributed by the
   hash code of (SYSDBA.p.state_born_id) to all AMPs. Then we do a
   SORT to order Spool 2 by row hash. The size of Spool 2 is
   estimated with low confidence to be 2 rows (216 bytes). The
   estimated time for this step is 0.01 seconds.
5) We do an all-AMPs JOIN step from SYSDBA.s by way of a RowHash
   match scan, which is joined to Spool 2 (Last Use) by way of a
```

```
RowHash match scan.  SYSDBA.s and Spool 2 are joined using a merge
join, with a join condition of ("state_born_id = SYSDBA.s.state_id").
The result goes into Spool 1 (group_amps), which is built locally
on the AMPs.  The size of Spool 1 is estimated with index join
confidence to be 2 rows (588 bytes).  The estimated time for this
step is 0.05 seconds.
```

Q: You used the phrase "one way Teradata", are there other mechanisms utilized by Teradata to resolve this distribution issue?

A: Looking at the process we just explained, you should quickly realize that redistributing a large table could require a lot of resources. In the case where one of the tables in the join is large and the other is small we could utilize another strategy. A full copy of the smaller table could be duplicated on all of the AMPs. Again the AMPs would have all the data they require locally, however in this case the large table's data did not have to be redistributed.

To show an example we have a table CarClub which has 5000 rows. The YearSmall table contains a single row. If we execute a query joining these two tables it would not make sense to redistribute the entire CarClub table.

```
select * from CarClub c, YearSmall y where CarYear = RefYear
```

Reviewing the explain plan we see in Step 4 that Teradata creates a copy of the YearSmall table into Spool 2 and duplicates it on all the AMPs. In Step 5, the CarClub table is joined with the Spool 2 table locally.

```
4) We do an all-AMPs RETRIEVE step from SYSDBA.y by way of an
      all-rows scan with a condition of ("NOT (SYSDBA.y.RefYear IS NULL)")
      into Spool 2 (all_amps), which is duplicated on all AMPs.  The
      size of Spool 2 is estimated with low confidence to be 4 rows (68
      bytes).  The estimated time for this step is 0.03 seconds.
5) We do an all-AMPs JOIN step from Spool 2 (Last Use) by way of an
      all-rows scan, which is joined to SYSDBA.c by way of an all-rows
      scan.  Spool 2 and SYSDBA.c are joined using a single partition
      hash_ join, with a join condition of ("SYSDBA.c.CarYear = RefYear").
      The result goes into Spool 1 (group_amps), which is built locally
      on the AMPs.  The size of Spool 1 is estimated with index join
      confidence to be 5,006 rows (2,382,856 bytes).  The estimated time
      for this step is 0.30 seconds.
```

Q: How does Teradata decide which method to use?

A: The Teradata optimizer works hard to create the most efficient execution plan for the query submitted. Based on what the query is trying to accomplish and the statistics collected on the tables the optimizer attempts to create the best possible method of execution.

Q: It is very interesting how the Teradata optimizer works to build the execution plan for a query. Is the optimizer smart enough to generate the same execution plan for different SQL constructs that accomplish the same thing?

A: In most cases the SQL you write has direct bearing on the execution plan generated.

Here is a classic example of a common SQL statement that; in the past has been a major performance issue when executed in Teradata.

When we first start to explore an existing database, one of the common things to do is to profile particular columns to determine what different values the column contains.

As an example, if we wanted to see what values were stored in the GENDER column in the CUSTOMER table, we might execute a SQL statement such as:

```
select distinct gender from customer
```

This is a pretty normal and straight forward SQL statement. However if we look how Teradata would execute this in older versions of Teradata we see an interesting execution plan.

```
Exlain select distinct gender from customer
3) We do an all-AMPs RETRIEVE step from FINANCIAL.customer by way of
   an all-rows scan with no residual conditions into Spool 1
   (group_amps), which is redistributed by hash code to all AMPs.
   Then we do a SORT to order Spool 1 by the sort key in spool field1
   eliminating duplicate rows.  The size of Spool 1 is estimated with
   low confidence to be 1,000 rows.  The estimated time for this step
   is 0.03 seconds.
```

Basically what Teradata is doing is to redistribute the table based on the gender column. In this example the gender column only has 2 values. Based on what we already know, this means at most only 2 AMPs will receive any data. This large data skew across the AMPs restricts the parallel processing for this task. Executing this SQL on a large table can be an extremely inefficient operation.

As an alternative, the SQL statement below returns the same results as the previous SELECT DISTINCT statement. When we analyize this execution plan we see a totally different approach.

```
Exlain select gender from customer group by gender
3) We do an all-AMPs SUM step to aggregate from FINANCIAL.customer by
   way of an all-rows scan with no residual conditions, and the
   grouping identifier in field 1030.  Aggregate Intermediate Results
   are computed globally, then placed in Spool 3.  The size of Spool
   3 is estimated with no confidence to be 32 rows.  The estimated
   time for this step is 0.04 seconds.
4) We do an all-AMPs RETRIEVE step from Spool 3 (Last Use) by way of
   an all-rows scan into Spool 1 (group_amps), which is built locally
   on the AMPs.  The size of Spool 1 is estimated with no confidence
   to be 32 rows.  The estimated time for this step is 0.04 seconds.
```

Here each AMP first aggregates the rows that it has stored. Having all the AMPs on the server performing this in parallel results in a much more efficient method of determining the unique values of the column.

Q: That was an interesting example to walk through. It really drove home the point of how valuable it is to really understand what is happening in the explain plan. You stated that this "was" be an issue in Teradata, what changed?

A: Doing a SELECT DISTINCT was such a common occurance that Teradata developers included logic to identify the request but create the more efficient execution plan of the GROUP BY method.

Current versions of Teradata will return the same execution plan for both SQL varations. While this removes this possible performance gotcha for this instance, there exists many other scenarios that will not be identified.

When you encounter a poor performing SQL, analyzing the explain plan and understanding what Teradata is trying to accomplish is the best 1st step in coming up with a better executing statement.

Compression

Q: With the rate of table growth these days, there is a lot of interest in being able to compress data in a database. Does Teradata provide any compression options?
A: Yes indeed. Teradata provides an option at the table level to compress data. It works a little different than other vendors approach and is basically an implementation with little drawbacks. A totally win-win solution.

Q: Come on, compression is always a balancing act. The higher level of compression the more CPU resources are required to compress and de-compress the data. Doesn't Teradata compress data like it is done, for example, in the ZIP application? What super-secret method does Teradata utilize that everyone else doesn't?
A: First you need to specify the COMPRESS definition when the table is created. The column definition section of the CREATE TABLE command allows for a COMPRESS attribute to be specified. Here a list of values for that column is defined. These values are then stored in the table header. When a row is created instead of storing the actual value, the row just references the value in the header.

Q: It really sounds more like a substitution concept than a compression implementation. Does this actually provide for smaller space utilization?
A: I guess the best way to illustrate the benefits of Teradata's compression implementation is to work through an example.

Assume we have a simple table CarClub which has the following definition:

```
CREATE SET TABLE CarClub (
      Car_id      INTEGER,
      CarYear     INTEGER,
      CarMake     CHAR(20),
      CarOwner    VARCHAR(1024)
PRIMARY INDEX ( Car_id );
```

The table has been populated with 5000 records that has a data profile as shown below.

Column	Number Nulls		Distinct Values	Min Value	Max Value	Min Length	Max Length
Car_id	0	(0%)	5000	1	5000	-	-
CarYear	190	(3%)	31	1983	2012	-	-
CarMake	346	(6%)	44		Volkswagen	0	13
CarOwner	351	(7%)	101		Young	0	10

After the table is populated, checking the table size shows a table that is 263,168 bytes in size.

Q: Ok, so now that we have a table to work with, how do I specify I want the table compressed?
A: Here is the actual syntax for the COMPRESS portion of the create table definition.

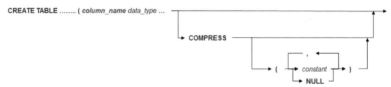

Maybe looking at an actual table definition with compression defined will make it easier to understand. First we will create a table where the just nulls are compressed from the CarYear and CarOwner columns. After the CarClub_CompressNulls table is created we insert all the uncompressed records from CarClub.

```
CREATE SET TABLE CarClub_CompressedNulls (
       Car_id INTEGER,
       CarYear INTEGER COMPRESS ,
       CarMake CHAR(20) COMPRESS ,
       CarOwner VARCHAR(1024))
PRIMARY INDEX ( Car_id );

Insert into CarClub_CompressedNulls select * from CarClub;
```

The new table is 255,488 bytes in size. This results in about a 2.9 percent reduction in size.

Q: That is not a huge savings but I guess it is something. However, I was expecting a much greater compression result.
A: As we can see compressing null values for a column save a small amount of space but we can realize real saving by compressing out the most commonly occurring values from the columns.

Expanding on our example, we now create a new table where we list common values in the COMPRESS definition for the two columns.

Notice that the values must be specified exactly as they are stored in the table. For the CarMake column, since it is a fixed length string data type, we must include the column's trailing spaces.

Again, we populate the compressed table with values from the initial CarClub table.

```
CREATE SET TABLE CarClub_CompressedMax (
      Car_id   INTEGER,
      CarYear  INTEGER COMPRESS (1983 ,1984 ,1985 ,1986 ,1987 ,1988 ,1989
                                ,1990 ,1991 ,1992 ,1993 ,1994 ,1995 ,1996
                                ,1997 ,1998 ,1999 ,2000 ,2001 ,2002 ,2003
                                ,2004 ,2005 ,2006 ,2007 ,2008 ,2009 ,2010
                                ,2011 ,2012 ),
      CarMake  CHAR(20) COMPRESS
                ('Acura                ','Aston Martin        ',
                 'Audi                 ','BMW                 ',
                 'Bentley              ','Buick               ',
                 'Cadillac             ','Chevrolet           ',
                 'Chrysler             ','Dodge               ',
                 'Ferrari              ','Fiat                ',
                 'Ford                 ','GMC                 ',
                 'Honda                ','Hyundai             ',
                 'Infiniti             ','Jaguar              ',
                 'Jeep                 ','Kia                 ',
                 'Lamborghini          ','Land Rover          ',
                 'Lexus                ','Lincoln             ',
                 'Lotus                ','MINI                ',
                 'Maserati             ','Mazda               ',
                 'McLaren              ','Mercedes-Benz       ',
                 'Mitsubishi           ','Nissan              ',
                 'Porsche              ','RAM                 ',
                 'Rolls-Royce          ','Scion               ',
                 'Smart                ','Subaru              ',
                 'Suzuki               ','Tesla               ',
                 'Toyota               ','Volkswagen          '),
      CarOwner VARCHAR(1024) CHARACTER SET LATIN NOT CASESPECIFIC)
PRIMARY INDEX ( Car_id );

Insert into CarClub_CompressedMax select * from CarClub;
```

By compressing the values specified in the CarYear and CarMake columns, the size of the CarClub_CompressedMax table takes up only 153,600 bytes. This results in a 41.6 percent reduction in space allocation.

Q: Well that is more like it. So we were able to reduce the amount of space by over half and we do not take a performance hit when accessing the data, which is pretty incredible.
A: It is actually even better than you think. By reducing the size of a row of data that means we get more rows in each data block. This gives us a performance boast when we access the table. Less space and better performance, a total win-win.

Q: I have a couple of questions though. First why didn't we also compress the CarOwner column?
A: I am sure you could have guessed that there would be some restrictions. Teradata compression does not allow for the compression of variable string columns.

Q: Does this mean compression is basically of no value for a table where the majority of the columns are defined as VARCHAR
A: Not at all. However it does mean that you may need to do some analysis before determining what data type would provide for the best implementation.

In our previous example, the CarMake column had 44 distinct values and the maximum length was 13 bytes long. If we created another table that just contains the Car_id and CarMake columns and populate it with the same data as before, we end up with a table occupying 193,024 Bytes.

```
CREATE SET TABLE CarChar (
      Car_id INTEGER,
      CarMake CHAR(20) )
PRIMARY INDEX ( Car_id );
```

Now if we create the table where CarMake is defined as a VARCHAR data type it reduces the size of the table to 144,896 bytes.

```
CREATE SET TABLE CarVarchar (
      Car_id INTEGER,
      CarMake VARCHAR(20) )
PRIMARY INDEX ( Car_id );
```

If we think about this, it makes sense. By storing the data as a variable string we can eliminate all the trailing spaces that get padded on when the column is fixed length.

Now let us look at another possibility. We go back and define the CarMake column as a fixed length CHAR data type and include the top occuring values in the compression defination.

```
CREATE SET TABLE CarCharCompressed (
      Car_id INTEGER,
      CarMake CHAR(20) COMPRESS
                  ('Acura              ','Aston Martin        ',
                   'Audi               ','BMW                 ',
                   'Bentley            ','Buick               ',
                   'Cadillac           ','Chevrolet           ',
                   'Chrysler           ','Dodge               ',
                   'Ferrari            ','Fiat                ',
                   'Ford               ','GMC                 ',
                   'Honda              ','Hyundai             ',
                   'Infiniti           ','Jaguar              ',
                   'Jeep               ','Kia                 ',
                   'Lamborghini        ','Land Rover          ',
                   'Lexus              ','Lincoln             ',
                   'Lotus              ','MINI                ',
                   'Maserati           ','Mazda               ',
                   'McLaren            ','Mercedes-Benz       ',
                   'Mitsubishi         ','Nissan              ',
                   'Porsche            ','RAM                 ',
                   'Rolls-Royce        ','Scion               ',
                   'Smart              ','Subaru              ',
                   'Suzuki             ','Tesla               ',
                   'Toyota             ','Volkswagen          ')
PRIMARY INDEX ( Car_id );
```

After populating the table we end up with a table size of 106,496 bytes. Using compression we end up with a table that is more than 25% smaller than the table that utilized a variable data type.

Weather you can utilize compression will depend on the specific characteristics of your data. For example, having a small number of distinct values in a column should be an indicator that the column needs futher study to see how well it will perform as a compressed column.

Also keep in mind that compressed strings are case senstive. If you define a compression value as "Ford" and insert "FORD" into a row, the column will not be compressed.

Q: In all of your examples you created a new table and then populated the table with data from the original table. Could I not just use an ALTER TABLE command?
A: Unfortunately no. You can only define compression attributes when the table is initially created.

Identity Columns

Q: Does Teradata have the equivalant of Oracle's sequence object? I tend to use sequences a lot in Oracle to generate surrogate key values.
A: Teradata does not have a sequence object. However it does implement the concept of an IDENTITY column similar to Microsoft SQL server or IBM's DB2.

A column can be defined with an identity property where when a row is inserted into the table, the value for that column will be automatically generated.

The syntax for defining an IDENTITY column as part of the create table command is shown below.

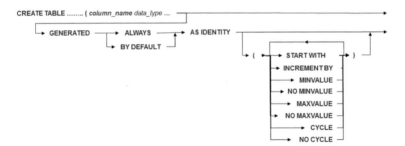

Q: Again with the crazy syntax diagrams. How about an example.?
A: Of course, a simple example will go a long way in explaining how an IDENTITY column is defined and utilized.

In this example we will create a table that stores a list of pet types (i.e. Dog, Cat, Fish etc.). To keep it simple the table will just contain an Id column and the name of the pet type. We would like to automatically generate the Id column using an IDENTITY column.

Our SQL statement would look like:

```
create table PetType (PetType_id integer generated always as identity,
                       PetTypeName Varchar(1024))
```

Now, if we insert some pet types into the table, the PetType_id column will be automatically assigned the next value.

```
insert into PetType (PetTypeName) values ('DOG');
insert into PetType (PetTypeName) values ('CAT');
insert into PetType (PetTypeName) values ('FISH');

select * from PetType order by 1
```

PetType_id	PetTypeName
1	DOG
2	CAT
3	FISH

Q: In your example you did not specify the PetType_id column in your insert statement and it assigned the value as I would have hoped. What happens if I do specify a value for an IDENTITY column?

A: It depends on how you defined the identity column. As in our example if you specified "... generated always..." whatever value you specified will be ignored and the next identity value assigned.

```
insert into PetType (PetType_Id, PetTypeName) values (9, 'BIRD');

select * from PetType order by 1
```

PetType_id	PetTypeName
1	DOG
2	CAT
3	FISH
4	BIRD

So even though on the insert statement we specified a value of 9 for the PetType_id column, the next identity value (of 4) was assigned.

Now on the other hand if we created our table as "...generated by default..." a value will be automatically assigned only if no value is specified.

If we execute the same insert commands into a table where the IDENTITY column has been defined as "generated by default" we now see that the PetType_id column has the value that we specified.

```
create table PetTypeDefault (
            PetType_id integer generated by default as identity,
            PetTypeName Varchar(1024) );

insert into PetTypeDefault (PetTypeName) values ('DOG');
insert into PetTypeDefault (PetTypeName) values ('CAT');
insert into PetTypeDefault (PetTypeName) values ('FISH');

insert into PetTypeDefault (PetType_Id, PetTypeName) values (9, 'BIRD');

select * from PetTypeDefault order by 1
```

PetType_id	PetTypeName
1	DOG
2	CAT
3	FISH
9	BIRD

Q: That works the way I would have imagined it would. What happens if I specify a value and then insert a row where the next

identity column value is already in the table? Does it skip over that value?

A: Unfortunately the IDENTITY column logic is not that smart. As shown below, you will end up with two rows with the same PetType_id

```
insert into PetTypeDefault values (4, 'RAT - Assigned');
insert into PetTypeDefault (PetTypeName) values ('RAT - Identity');

select * from PetTypeDefault order by 1
PetType_id  PetTypeName
1           DOG
2           CAT
3           FISH
4           RAT - Assigned
4           RAT - Identity
9           BIRD
```

If you are going to use the "generated by default" option you need to be very careful of what values get assigned to avoid having duplicate entities.

Q: The remaining options seem pretty straight forward. The "Start with", "Increment by", "MinValue" and "MaxValue" all make sense but what about the "Cycle" option. How does that work?

A: The "Cycle" option specifies that if the identity value reaches the MaxValue amount then cycle the identity value back to what was specified for MinValue.

Here we define an IDENTITY column that starts with the value of 1 and a maximum value of 3. In addition the IDENTITY column values are specified to cycle values.

The first three rows get assign the values 1 through 3, however when we go to insert the "Bird" row the value assigned to PetType_id has been cycled back to 1.

```
create table PetTypeCycle (
             PetType_id integer generated always as identity
                        (start with 1 MinValue 1 MaxValue 3 Cycle),
             PetTypeName Varchar(1024));

insert into PetTypeCycle (PetTypeName) values ('DOG');
insert into PetTypeCycle (PetTypeName) values ('CAT');
insert into PetTypeCycle (PetTypeName) values ('FISH');

insert into PetTypeCycle (PetTypeName) values ('BIRD');

select * from PetTypeCycle order by 1
PetType_id  PetTypeName
1           BIRD
1           DOG
2           CAT
3           FISH
```

As with generating identity values by default, cycling identity values can lead to unexpected duplicates being generated.

Q: Can I use an ALTER TABLE SQL statement to add an IDENTITY column to an existing table?

A: Similar to the compression attribute, IDENTITY columns can only be specified on a CREATE TABLE command.

No Primary Index

Q: I am reading the title for this section and thinking what is going on here, so far you have kept saying that every table is Teradata has to have a Primary Index. What gives?
A: I need to apologize. In the vast majority of the cases it is true that every table in Teradata has to have a Primary Index defined. However, Teradata recently has implemented an option where we can actually define a table without specifying a Primary Index (referred to as NoPI table).

Q: Why would your want to do that and more importantly if you did define a table without a Primary Index how does the data get distributed?
A: In some instances we could have a set of data that doesn't have a good option to utilize as a Primary Index. When loading external data into a Teradata database it is becoming a best practice just to load the raw data and then perform the transformations within the database (ELT).

When implementing such a process it would be more efficient to just bypass the whole Primary Index processing and just randomly assign a data row to an AMP. From that point we could perform any transformations on the data required as we move to it final destination.

For example if I needed to load some bulk Car information as shown in the table below, it is possible that none of the 3 columns would work efficiently as a Primary Index. So as an option I can create the table without a Primary Index.

```
CREATE TABLE CarsRAW       (
     CarYear    INTEGER,
     CarMake    CHAR(100),
     CarOwner   VARCHAR(1024)  )
NO PRIMARY INDEX ;
```

Now when I populate the table the rows are randomly and equally distributed across the available AMPs.

Q: You kept saying that I always need to come up with an efficient Primary Index for all my tables. This seems easier, why can't I just define all my tables as NO PRIMARY INDEX?
A:Because of course there are a number of restrictions. As you now know that the Primary Index not only provides a mechanism for data distribution but also for quickly locating the row in the table.

Without a Primary Index defined all table accesses will become all AMP, full table scans. When as part of a load process this is not usually a big issue as all the rows are most likely going to be processed.

We can see this by looking at the explain plan of a query that wants to access a specific sub-set of the table.

```
select * from CarsRAW where CarMake = 'Ford'
  3) We do an all-AMPs RETRIEVE step from SYSDBA.CarsRAW by way of an
     all-rows scan with a condition of ("SYSDBA.CarsRAW.CarMake = 'Ford
     '") into Spool 1 (group_amps), which is built locally on the AMPs.
     The size of Spool 1 is estimated with no confidence to be 500 rows
     (234,000 bytes).  The estimated time for this step is 0.07 seconds.
```

Q: Isn't there any way I can avoid a full table scan. I can see a case where I may need to perform a transformation on selected rows in a table. With loading data the volumes tend to be large, so doing a full table scan could be an issue.
A: You can create secondary indexes on NoPI tables to provide an efficient direct path to a row or set of rows.

Q: Do any of the Teradata load utilities support loading data into NoPI tables.
A: Yes, FastLoad and TPump can utilize No Primary Index tables to provide increased performance.

Q: Any other interesting aspects of NoPI tables?
A: There are a lot of specifics associated with NoPI tables and additional research will assist with a particular implementation.

However, one final note is that all NoPI tables are defined as MULTISET. If you try and define a NoPI table as a SET table you will receive an error.

```
CREATE SET TABLE CarsRAW        (
     CarYear    INTEGER,
     CarMake    CHAR(100),
     CarOwner   VARCHAR(1024) )
NO PRIMARY INDEX ;
Syntax error: Cannot create a NoPI table as a SET table.
```

NoPI tables can greatly enhance processing especially when utilized in loading and staging applications.

Copy Table

Q: How can I create a copy of an existing table in Teradata?
A: There are a number of ways to accomplish that in Teradata. One method would be to use a "CREATE TABLE as (SELECT ..." statement.

Q: Many of the other databases I work support a "CREATE TABLE as" operation, However when I tried the same syntax on Teradata, I received an error message.

```
Create table CarClubCopy as (select * from CarClub)
Syntax error: expected something between ')' and ';'
```

Q: What am I missing?

A: Teradata has an additional option to specify if we want the new table populated with data or created with the same structure but left empty. To create a copy the CarClub table and populate the new table with data we would execute:

```
Create table CarClubCopy as (select * from CarClub) with data;
```

To create an empty copy of the CarClub table structure, we would specify the **with no data** option.

```
Create table CarClubCopy as (select * from CarClub) with no data;
```

Q: You implied that there was another method to create a copy of a table. Care to enlighten us?

A: As part of the "CREATE TABLE" command, Teradata implements an option "as" to create the new table as a copy of a specified table.

```
Create table CarClubAS as CarClub with data;
```

Q: So what is the difference between the two methods? It appears that both ways end up with the same result.

A: There are actually some subtle differences between the two methods. To illustrate, first, let us create an secondary index on the CarClub table. After the index is created, we will make a copies of the CarClub table using each method.

```
Create index CarClubNUSI (CarOwner) on CarClub;

Create table CarClubCopySelect as (select * from CarClub) with data;

Create table CarClubCopyAs as CarClub with data;
```

Now using the "SHOW TABLE" command we can view the table structure that was created. First we look at the table that was created using the create/select method:

```
show table CarClubCopySelect;
CREATE SET TABLE SYSDBA.CarClubCopySelect ,NO FALLBACK ,
     NO BEFORE JOURNAL,
     NO AFTER JOURNAL,
     CHECKSUM = DEFAULT
     (
      Car_id INTEGER,
      CarYear INTEGER,
      CarMake CHAR(100) CHARACTER SET LATIN NOT CASESPECIFIC,
      CarOwner VARCHAR(1024) CHARACTER SET LATIN NOT CASESPECIFIC)
PRIMARY INDEX ( Car_id );
```

And now the table created with the Create/As method.

```
show table CarClubCopyAs;
CREATE SET TABLE SYSDBA.CarClubCopyAs ,NO FALLBACK ,
     NO BEFORE JOURNAL,
     NO AFTER JOURNAL,
     CHECKSUM = DEFAULT
     (
      Car_id INTEGER,
```

```
      CarYear INTEGER,
      CarMake CHAR(100) CHARACTER SET LATIN NOT CASESPECIFIC,
      CarOwner VARCHAR(1024) CHARACTER SET LATIN NOT CASESPECIFIC)
PRIMARY INDEX ( Car_id )
INDEX CarClubNUSI ( CarOwner );
```

You should notice that the table created with the Create/As method maintained the secondary index we add. However that index was not created using the Create/Select method.

As shown in this example, a number of the properties of a table will not be created in the new copy of the table when using the Create/Select method.

Teradata Indexes

Q: I keep hearing Teradata people talk about UPI, NUPI, USI, NUSI, and PPI when referring to indexes, what does this jargon mean?
A: Indexes in Teradata are implemented differently than in many other databases. The acronyms that you mention refer to:

UPI	Unique Primary Index
NUPI	Non-Unique Primary Index
USI	Unique Secondary Index
NUSI	Non-Unique Secondary Index
PPI	Partitioned Primary Index

We have talked about Primary Indexes in the previous section on tables, so in this section we will focus on the other types of indexes available in Teradata.

Secondary Indexes

Q: Why this specific differentiation between unique and non-unique secondary indexes? Does it really make that much difference?
A: Teradata actually handles unique secondary indexes much differently than non-unique secondary indexes. Both types of secondary indexes are stored as sub-tables. The indexes using the hashing concept to store and then look up values.

The index is basically a table where the Primary index is the index column(s) and it contains a column that is the row id of where that row is located in the base table.

In the case of a Unique Secondary index we know that we can find at most a single row and that row will reside on a single AMP.

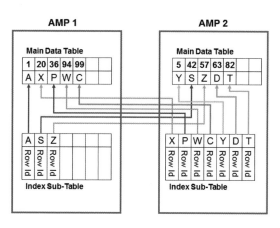

The steps in accessing a row via a USI are:

- HASH the index columns to obtain the AMP the index entry resides on.
- Have that AMP lookup the entry and return the row location of the data in the base table.
- Using the row id, have the associated AMP return the data.

Since in most cases, the index entry and the base table data will be located on different AMPs, the data access will involve two AMPs. While this is twice the cost in performance as accessing a row using a UPI, it is still an efficient operation.

To show an example that will validate the USI process we will define a simple table VACATIONS and then create a Unique Secondary Index on the LocationId column of the table.

```
CREATE SET TABLE Vacations (
      VacationId         INTEGER,
      LocationId         INTEGER,
      DepartureDate DATE FORMAT)
PRIMARY INDEX ( VacationId );

create unique index VacationsUSI (LocationId) on Vacations;
```

Querying the table selecting a specific LocationId value we obtain the following explain plan.

```
Select * from Vacations where LocationId = 2
1) First, we do a two-AMP RETRIEVE step from SYSDBA.Vacations by way
   of unique index # 4 "SYSDBA.Vacations.LocationId = 2" with no
   residual conditions.  The estimated time for this step is 0.01
   seconds.
```

The explain plan details that Teradata is will use the Unique Index we created to access the row we requested. The process will engage one AMP to access the index sub-table to find the location of the target row and then engage another AMP to fetch the final result.

Q: So why would having duplicate index entries change things?
A: The problem is in the hashing of the index values. While all of the index values that are the same would go to the same AMP, the link to the base table data would be spread out across all the other AMPs.

To solve this issue, NUSI indexes are implemented on each AMP. An index sub-table exists on each AMP that contains entries only for the rows that reside on that AMP.

The diagram below illustrates this structure.

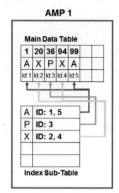 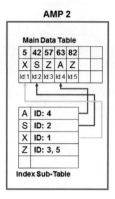

So in executing a query using a NUSI, all AMPs are involved in the process. Each AMP looks up the index value and then retrieves the data from the main table that resides on that AMP.

If we create a NUSI on the DepartureDate of our example VACATIONS table we can how this is accomplished.

```
create index VacationsNUSI (DepartureDate) on Vacations;
```

In the explain plan, Teradata details that the execution will include all-AMPs. Each AMP will use the NUSI that was created to locate the rows residing there and place them into a locally created Spool file. The Spool file will then be returned with the query's results.

```
select * from Vacations where DepartureDate = date'2013-01-01'
3) We do an all-AMPs RETRIEVE step from SYSDBA.Vacations by way of
   index # 4 "SYSDBA.Vacations.DepartureDate = DATE '2013-01-01'"
   with no residual conditions into Spool 1 (group_amps), which is
   built locally on the AMPs.  The size of Spool 1 is estimated with
   high confidence to be 19 rows (741 bytes).  The estimated time for
   this step is 0.08 seconds.
```

Q: I was following along with the examples. I created my own Vacations table, inserted a few rows and then created a NUSI index on the table.

```
CREATE SET TABLE myVacations (
      VacationId INTEGER,
      LocationId INTEGER,
      DepartureDate DATE)
PRIMARY INDEX ( VacationId );

insert into myVacations values (1,2, date'2013-01-01');
insert into myVacations values (2,3, date'1996-04-06');

CREATE INDEX myVacations_NUSI (DepartureDate) ON myVacations;
```

However, now when I generate an explain plan, that should use the index Teradata is telling me it is going to ignore the index and do a full table scan.

```
Select * from myVacations where DepartureDate = date'2013-01-01';
3) We do an all-AMPs RETRIEVE step from SYSDBA.myVacations by way of
   an all-rows scan with a condition of (
   "SYSDBA.myVacations.DepartureDate = DATE '2013-01-01'") into Spool
   1 (group_amps), which is built locally on the AMPs.  The size of
   Spool 1 is estimated with low confidence to be 2 rows (78 bytes).
   The estimated time for this step is 0.03 seconds.
```

Why doesn't the result from my query match what you presented?
A: A couple of issues are involved here. Teradata will always try to determine the fastest method to execute a query. In this case you only inserted 2 rows. Teradata knows that with only a few rows in a table it is faster to do a full table scan than to access the index and then the main table. In my example I inserted a few thousand rows.

Remember how we talked about statistics. To insure the Teradata optimizer has all the information necessary to create the optimal execution plan, we need to collect fresh statistics on the index.

Q: What is the full syntax for creating a secondary index?
A: To create an index on an existing table the following SQL can be utilized.

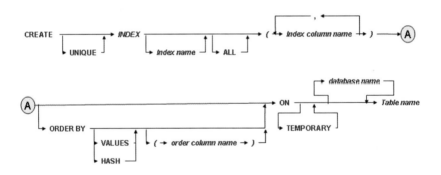

Q: Can my secondary indexes contain multiple columns?
A: Of course, but remember, just like Primary indexes all the columns in the index will be used in the Hashing to determine what AMP the index row will reside on.

Here we create a multi-column index on the LocationId and DeartureDate columns of the Vacations table.

```
CREATE INDEX Vacations_mcUSI (LocationId, DepartureDate) ON Vacations;
```

Now if the table is queried with both LocationId and DepartureDate values the NUSI will be used in the query.

```
select * from Vacations where LocationId = 12 and DepartureDate =
date'2013-01-01'
 3) We do an all-AMPs RETRIEVE step from SYSDBA.Vacations by way of
    index # 8 "SYSDBA.Vacations.LocationId = 12,
    SYSDBA.Vacations.DepartureDate = DATE '2013-01-01'" with no
    residual conditions into Spool 1 (group_amps), which is built
    locally on the AMPs. The size of Spool 1 is estimated with low
    confidence to be 3 rows (117 bytes). The estimated time for this
    step is 0.05 seconds.
```

However, just as with a multi-Column Primary Index, if only one of the
columns that make up the index is specified, the index is ignored and a full
table scan is preformed.

```
select * from Vacations where LocationId = 12
 3) We do an all-AMPs RETRIEVE step from SYSDBA.Vacations by way of an
    all-rows scan with a condition of ("SYSDBA.Vacations.LocationId =
    12") into Spool 1 (group_amps), which is built locally on the AMPs.
    The size of Spool 1 is estimated with no confidence to be 5,281
    rows (205,959 bytes). The estimated time for this step is 0.11
    seconds.
```

**Q: I noticed in your syntax diagram for the Secondary Index
creation that there is an option for something using an "ORDER BY"
phrase. What is that for?**
A: Remember that a Secondary Index is implemented as a sub-table of the
main table. By default, Teradata will create a non-unique secondary index as a
HASH-Ordered NUSI. To create the index sub-table the secondary index key
column(s) will be used to generate the HASH-Row Id value. Since there may be
duplicates the HASH-Row Id also contains a uniqueness component.

In this diagram, we illustrate the creation of a HASH-Ordered NUSI index.
Since for a NUSI each AMP builds the index table locally, the diagram is an
example for a single AMP.

In storing the rows of the index table the rows are stored based on the HASH-
Row Id. This makes locating a single value efficient.

In the creation of the NUSI, if the "Order by Value" option is specified, Teradata creates the index sub-table in the same manor as in the HASH-Ordered, however the rows are ordered by the column value.

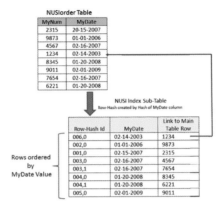

Setting up a NUSI as a Value-Ordered NUSI is especially useful in improving performance for SQL containing a BETWEEN range selection.

Q: Are there any limitations on creating a Value-Ordered NUSI?
A: The only data type allowed for the key on a Value-Ordered NUSI is an integer. The key must be a numeric value that is less than 4 bytes.

Partitioned Primary Index (PPI)

Q: In the list of indexes you showed at the beginning of this section, you indicated that there was an index called a Partitioned Primary Index. Does Teradata support partitioning?
A: In a way you can think of the Primary Index architecture as an implementation of HASH partitioning. You could think of the AMPs as partitions. Teradata automatically assigns the table's data to one of the AMPs and when a query is executed it may be able to eliminate AMPs (think partitions) from being included in the execution plan.

In addition, Teradata supports the ability to create a Partitioned Primary Index (PPI) to aid in reducing the amount of data required to be scanned.

To illustrate the use of a implementing a PPI table, we will use the simple table definition below:

```
CREATE TABLE OfficeVisits (
      PatientId      INTEGER,
      VisitDate      DATE,
      InsuranceCode INTEGER)
PRIMARY INDEX ( PatientId );
```

After populating the table with some sample data, we might see the following data stored on a single AMP.

AMP 1			
Row Hash	PatientId	VisitDate	InsuranceCode
nnn	10	01-05-2012	900
nnn	11	02-15-2012	811
nnn	12	03-25-2012	746
nnn	21	01-05-2012	900
nnn	25	02-15-2012	811
nnn	26	03-25-2012	746
nnn	33	01-05-2012	900
nnn	36	02-15-2012	811
nnn	39	03-25-2012	746

If we wanted to retrieve all the rows where the InsuranceCode is equal 811 we could execute the following SQL.

```
select * from OfficeVisits where InsuranceCode = 811
```

In this case there are no Secondary Indexes on the table and our WHERE condition is on the InsuranceCode column which is not the Primary Index. This forces Teradata to perform a full table scan on all the AMPs.

This is shown in the explain plan for the query.

```
3) We do an all-AMPs RETRIEVE step from SYSDBA.OfficeVisits by way of
   an all-rows scan with a condition of (
   "SYSDBA.OfficeVisits.InsuranceCode = 811") into Spool 1
   (group_amps), which is built locally on the AMPs.  The size of
   Spool 1 is estimated with high confidence to be 3 rows (117 bytes).
   The estimated time for this step is 0.03 seconds.
```

Q: Yes, that is pretty much what I expected. How does partitioning help to eliminate the full table scan?
A: Partitioning can make our query more efficient by grouping all of the same InsuranceCode values together into a single partition on each of the AMPs.

Here we create a table using a partitioning-clause to specify that we want to partition the data by InsuranceCode.

```
CREATE TABLE OfficeVisitsPPI (
      PatientId       INTEGER,
      VisitDate       DATE,
      InsuranceCode   INTEGER)
PRIMARY INDEX ( PatientId )
PARTITION BY InsuranceCode ;
```

Now when the data is organized on each AMP we keep all of the rows with the same InsuranceCode values in their own partition. For a partitioned table the rows are referenced first by their partition number and then the Row HASH.

Our previous data example would be organized similar to the diagram below.

AMP 1				
Partition Number	Row Hash	PatientId	VisitDate	InsuranceCode
1	nnn	12	03-25-2012	746
1	nnn	26	03-25-2012	746
1	nnn	39	03-25-2012	746
2	nnn	11	02-15-2012	811
2	nnn	25	02-15-2012	811
2	nnn	36	02-15-2012	811
3	nnn	10	01-05-2012	900
3	nnn	21	01-05-2012	900
3	nnn	33	01-05-2012	900

Now if we executed the same query against the table with the PPI, we would get the following execution plan.

```
select * from OfficeVisitsPPI where InsuranceCode = 811
  3) We do an all-AMPs RETRIEVE step from a single partition of
     SYSDBA.OfficeVisitsPPI with a condition of (
     "SYSDBA.OfficeVisitsPPI.InsuranceCode = 811") with a residual
     condition of ("SYSDBA.OfficeVisitsPPI.InsuranceCode = 811") into
     Spool 1 (group_amps), which is built locally on the AMPs. The
     size of Spool 1 is estimated with high confidence to be 3 rows (
     117 bytes). The estimated time for this step is 0.03 seconds.
```

Now each of the AMPs can go directly to the partition containing the 811 values and create the result set.

Q: You refer to Teradata's partitioning as a Partitioned Primary Index; is there a Unique Partitioned Primary Index as well as a Non-Unique Partitioned Primary Index?

A: In most cases creating a table with a Unique Partitioned Primary Index does not make a lot of sense and there is a serious restriction that limits where it can be implemented.

In order to use the UNIQUE keyword when creating a Partitioned Primary Index the partitioning column must be part of the Primary Index. So Teradata would allow me to create a table like the one below but it doesn't make much sense. Each row would be in its own partition and with a plain Unique Primary Index on PatientId, Teradata would be able to directly get to the row anyway.

```
CREATE TABLE OfficeVisitsUPPI (
     PatientId       INTEGER,
     VisitDate       DATE,
     InsuranceCode   INTEGER)
unique PRIMARY INDEX ( PatientId )
PARTITION BY PatientId ;
```

Q: Ok, so for the most part the Partitioned Primary Index is going to be Non-Unique. However, just for my curiosity, any clue why Teradata has this restriction?
A: To better illustrate how this could be an issue, let's go back to our original OfficeVisitsPPI table. This time let use look at the explain plan if we executed a query looking for a specific PatientId value.

```
select * from OfficeVisitsPPI where PatientId = 12
  1) First, we do a single-AMP RETRIEVE step from all partitions of
     SYSDBA.OfficeVisitsPPI by way of the primary index
     "SYSDBA.OfficeVisitsPPI.PatientId = 12" with a residual condition
     of ("SYSDBA.OfficeVisitsPPI.PatientId = 12") into Spool 1
     (one-amp), which is built locally on that AMP. The size of Spool
     1 is estimated with high confidence to be 2 rows (78 bytes). The
     estimated time for this step is 0.02 seconds.
```

Looking back at the previous diagram showing how the partitioned table is organized, we notice that the rows are arranged by partition number then the Primary Index row HASH value.

While we can identify which AMP will contain the row we want, we still have to check every partition to see if that partition contains the row we want.

In this case if we allowed the Primary Index to be unique, every row inserted would need to do this expensive validation to insure the row didn't already exist.

Q: I can understand the performance issue involved here but not allowing a unique PPI in this situation just seems to be a sneaky way to avoid the issue when querying the PPI table by the Primary Index.

Even with a non-unique PPI is there any way I can get around this performance issue? Also, what if I have the requirement to insure the Primary Index is unique, am I just out of luck?
A: Actually no. Secondary Indexes can be created on PPI tables. A Unique Secondary Index can be created on our table. Not only will this insure that the Primary Index values remain unique but also improve query performance.

```
CREATE SET TABLE sysDBA.OfficeVisitsPPIwI  (
      PatientId     INTEGER,
      VisitDate     DATE,
      InsuranceCode INTEGER)
PRIMARY INDEX ( PatientId )
PARTITION BY InsuranceCode
UNIQUE INDEX OfficeVisitsPPIwI_USI ( PatientId );

insert into  OfficeVisitsPPIwI values (12, date'2012-03-25', 746);
1 Rows Inserted
insert into  OfficeVisitsPPIwI values (12, date'2012-03-25', 746);
Secondary index uniqueness violation in sysDBA.OfficeVisitsPPIwI.
```

In the example above we validate that the USI insures that the Primary Index remains unique.

In addition if we query the table based on a Primary Index value, Teradata no longer has to search all the table partitions on that AMP but can use the USI to locate the row.

```
select * from OfficeVisitsPPIwI where PatientId = 12
  1) First, we do a two-AMP RETRIEVE step from SYSDBA.OfficeVisitsPPIwI
     by way of unique index # 4 "SYSDBA.OfficeVisitsPPIwI.PatientId =
     12" with no residual conditions. The estimated time for this step
     is 0.01 seconds.
```

The query is now a two-AMP operation.

Q: What about the partitions themselves. In the CREATE TABLE SQL, we didn't specifically define the partitions. How did Teradata know what partitions we were going to require?
A: Teradata allows for a maximum of 65,535 partitions. Since the InsuranceCode partitioning column was an Integer, Teradata will use the value of the InsuranceCode as the partition number. However if we tried to insert a row with a value of zero or greater than 65,535 we would get an error.

```
insert into  OfficeVisitsPPIwI values (98, date'2012-03-25', 0);
Partitioning violation for table sysDBA.OfficeVisitsPPIwI.
insert into  OfficeVisitsPPIwI values (99, date'2012-03-25', 65536);
Partitioning violation for table sysDBA.OfficeVisitsPPIwI.
```

Q: That doesn't seem very flexible. Doesn't Teradata provide any better methods for defining partitions?
A: Of course. We just used the simplest possible partitioning method to introduce the partitioning concept. Teradata implements RANGE_N and CASE_N options for defining partitions.

To create an example of our office visit table partitioned on the VisitDate column we could use the following CREATE TABLE SQL.

```
CREATE SET TABLE sysDBA.OfficeVisitsPPI_R  (
       PatientId     INTEGER,
       VisitDate     DATE,
       InsuranceCode INTEGER)
PRIMARY INDEX ( PatientId )
PARTITION BY RANGE_N (VisitDate
       between date'2012-01-01' and date'2012-12-31' each interval '1' day)
```

In this case a partition is created in the table for each day of 2012. Basically each value defined in the range statement is mapped into a partition number.

When we do a query of the table where VisitDate is included in the WHERE clause, Teradata can map the date specified into its partition number. Using that partition number only that partition needs to be scanned. This eliminates the need to scan the entire table.

Viewing the explain plan for this query shows Teradata only scanning the single partition required.

```
select * from sysDBA.OfficeVisitsPPI_R where VisitDate = date'2012-03-25'
 3) We do an all-AMPs RETRIEVE step from a single partition of
    sysDBA.OfficeVisitsPPI_R with a condition of (
    "sysDBA.OfficeVisitsPPI_R.VisitDate = DATE '2012-03-25'") with a
    residual condition of ("sysDBA.OfficeVisitsPPI_R.VisitDate = DATE
    '2012-03-25'") into Spool 1 (group_amps), which is built locally
    on the AMPs. The size of Spool 1 is estimated with no confidence
    to be 1 row (39 bytes). The estimated time for this step is 0.03
    seconds.
```

Q: This is a more practical example of partitioning. Are there any limitations to the size of the range I can define?
A: Using the RANGE_N option still limits you to a maximum of 65,535 total partitions. If I try and define a range that would result in more than 65,535 partitions, the SQL would fail.

```
CREATE SET TABLE sysDBA.OfficeVisitsPPI_RX  (
     PatientId     INTEGER,
     VisitDate     DATE,
     InsuranceCode INTEGER)
PRIMARY INDEX ( PatientId )
PARTITION BY RANGE_N (VisitDate between date'1800-01-01'
                      and date'2012-12-31' each interval '1' day)
PARTITION BY RANGE_N defines more than 65533 ranges.
```

Q: Wait, you said I could have a maximum of 65,535 partitions but in your example the error message says I tried to create more than 65,533 partitions. Which is it?
A: Two part ions are reserved for special cases. There is a partition designated as NO RANGE (or NO CASE) for rows that do not match any of the range buckets and an UNKNOWN partition.

Our next example will utilize these options.

In addition to the ability to define partitions based on a range expression, we can also define partitions with a case statement structure.
In the definition of the table OfficeVisitsPPI_C we specify that we would like the table partitioned by InsuranceCode. Using the CASE_N option, the partitions are defined based upon a list of case like conditions.

```
CREATE SET TABLE sysDBA.OfficeVisitsPPI_C  (
     PatientId     INTEGER,
     VisitDate     DATE,
     InsuranceCode INTEGER)
PRIMARY INDEX ( PatientId )
PARTITION BY CASE_N (InsuranceCode < 100,
                     InsuranceCode < 300,
                     InsuranceCode < 400,
                     InsuranceCode < 500,
                     InsuranceCode < 900,
                     NO CASE,
                     UNKNOWN)
```

When the table is accessed selecting an InsuranceCode value, just like in the
range option example, the InsuranceCode is mapped to the correct partition
and then just that partitioned is scanned for rows to be selected.

```
select * from sysDBA.OfficeVisitsPPI_C where InsuranceCode = 850
  3) We do an all-AMPs RETRIEVE step from a single partition of
  sysDBA.OfficeVisitsPPI_C with a condition of (
  "sysDBA.OfficeVisitsPPI_C.InsuranceCode = 850") with a residual
  condition of ("sysDBA.OfficeVisitsPPI_C.InsuranceCode = 850") into
  Spool 1 (group_amps), which is built locally on the AMPs.  The
  size of Spool 1 is estimated with no confidence to be 1 row (39
  bytes).  The estimated time for this step is 0.03 seconds.
```

Q: For dealing with very large tables does Teradata allow for sub-partitions?

A: In Teradata they are usually referred to as a Multi-Level Partitioned Primary
Index. The OfficeVisits table could be partitioned with a range partitioning and
then within each range partition we create case partitioning based on
InsuranceCode.

```
CREATE TABLE sysDBA.OfficeVisitsMLPPI   (
        PatientId      INTEGER,
        VisitDate      DATE,
        InsuranceCode  INTEGER)
PRIMARY INDEX ( PatientId )
PARTITION BY (RANGE_N (VisitDate between date'2012-01-01' and date'2012-
12-31' each interval '1' day),
                CASE_N (InsuranceCode < 100,
                        InsuranceCode < 300,
                        InsuranceCode < 400,
                        InsuranceCode < 500,
                        InsuranceCode < 900,
                        NO CASE,
                        UNKNOWN)  )
```

This will reduce the size of each partition making queries looking for a specific
InsuranceCode on a specific date very efficient.

```
select * from sysDBA.OfficeVisitsMLPPI where VisitDate = date'2012-03-25'
                                     and InsuranceCode = 746
  3) We do an all-AMPs RETRIEVE step from a single partition of
  sysDBA.OfficeVisitsMLPPI with a condition of (
  "sysDBA.OfficeVisitsMLPPI.VisitDate = DATE '2012-03-25',
  sysDBA.OfficeVisitsMLPPI.InsuranceCode = 746") with a residual
  condition of ("(sysDBA.OfficeVisitsMLPPI.InsuranceCode = 746) AND
  (sysDBA.OfficeVisitsMLPPI.VisitDate = DATE '2012-03-25')") into
  Spool 1 (group_amps), which is built locally on the AMPs.  The
  size of Spool 1 is estimated with no confidence to be 1 row (39
  bytes).  The estimated time for this step is 0.03 seconds.
```

One thing to remember is that even with Multi Level Partitioned Primary
Indexing the maximum number of partitions is 65,535. Creating a range
partitioned table by day, requires 365 partitions for a single year. In the
example above each of the 365 partitions would have 7 case sub-partitions. This
would result in a total of 2,555 partitions.

Q: Looking at the Multi-Level Partitioned Primary Index example you presented above, if I did a query with the only condition being a specific date does the partitioning help at all?
A: It obviously will not be as efficient as if you specify an InsuranceCode with a date but Teradata can still eliminate all the partitions with a different date. Teradata will select the appropriate partition for the date specified but then it is forced to check all of the sub-partitions.

```
select * from sysDBA.OfficeVisitsMLPPI where VisitDate = date'2012-03-25'
 3) We do an all-AMPs RETRIEVE step from 7 partitions of
    sysDBA.OfficeVisitsMLPPI with a condition of (
    "sysDBA.OfficeVisitsMLPPI.VisitDate = DATE '2012-03-25'") into
    Spool 1 (group_amps), which is built locally on the AMPs. The
    size of Spool 1 is estimated with no confidence to be 1 row (39
    bytes). The estimated time for this step is 0.03 seconds.
```

Q: After I create a partitioned table and it gets populated with data, is there any way to see the data distribution across the partitions?
A: Teradata provides a pseudo-column called PARTITION that can be used in a SELECT statement to display the row count by partition.

```
select PARTITION, count(*) from OfficeVisitsPPI group by partition
PARTITION   Count(*)
900         3
746         3
468         3
811         3
382         3
```

This provides an excellent way to determine the efficiency of a particular partitioning scheme.

Join Indexes

Q: I think I have a handle on of what Teradata has available in regard to Primary, Partitioned and Secondary Indexes. Do any other types of Indexes exist in Teradata?
A: As a matter of fact, Teradata provides some unique Indexing options. One of these, the Join Index, is a powerful construct that can greatly increase the speed of accessing your data.

The Join Index can provide speed increases in cases where:
- Tables that are frequently joined can be pre-join and accessed through the Join Index.
- The Join Index can contain a sparse representation of the table data reducing the entries that must be traversed.
- The join index can contain pre-aggregated values.

Q: That sounds like it is really complicated and would take forever to create and maintain. Are these join indexes only valuable in very specific incidences?
A: While it is true that join indexes have a lot of options and do require some forethought in setting up, they are not the evil monster that they first appear.

Let's look at a simple example:

First we will create a couple of very simple tables and load some sample data.

```
CREATE SET TABLE potus
    (
        potus_id INTEGER,
        state_born_id INTEGER,
        name VARCHAR(256) )
PRIMARY INDEX ( potus_id );

INSERT INTO potus   Values (2,2,'John Adams');
INSERT INTO potus   Values (5,1,'James Monroe');
INSERT INTO potus   Values (7,3,'Andrew Jackson');
INSERT INTO potus   Values (4,1,'James Madison');
INSERT INTO potus   Values (1,1,'George Washington');
INSERT INTO potus   Values (3,1,'Thomas Jefferson');
INSERT INTO potus   Values (6,2,'John Quincy Adams');
```

```
CREATE SET TABLE state (
        state_id INTEGER,
        state_name VARCHAR(256),
        state_capital VARCHAR(256) )
UNIQUE PRIMARY INDEX ( state_id );

INSERT INTO potus   Values (2,'Massachusetts', 'Boston');
INSERT INTO potus   Values (3,'South Carolina', 'Columbia');
INSERT INTO potus   Values (1,'Virginia', 'Richmond');
```

Now if we wanted to get a list of the presidents and what state they were born in we might use a SQL statement similar to the one below. This SQL statement would produce an EXPLAIN plan as shown.

```
select
        name, state_name
from
        potus join state on state_id = state_born_id
4) We do an all-AMPs RETRIEVE step from SYSDBA.potus by way of an
   all-rows scan with a condition of ("NOT
   (SYSDBA.potus.state_born_id IS NULL)") into Spool 2 (all_amps),
   which is redistributed by the hash code of (
   SYSDBA.potus.state_born_id) to all AMPs.  Then we do a SORT to
   order Spool 2 by row hash.  The size of Spool 2 is estimated with
   no confidence to be 13 rows (1,352 bytes).  The estimated time for
   this step is 0.01 seconds.
5) We do an all-AMPs JOIN step from SYSDBA.state by way of a RowHash
   match scan, which is joined to Spool 2 (Last Use) by way of a
   RowHash match scan.  SYSDBA.state and Spool 2 are joined using a
   merge join, with a join condition of ("SYSDBA.state.state_id =
   state_born_id").  The result goes into Spool 1 (group_amps), which
   is built locally on the AMPs.  The size of Spool 1 is estimated
   with no confidence to be 16 rows (3,120 bytes).  The estimated
   time for this step is 0.05 seconds.
```

If we analyze the EXPLAIN plan, we see that Teradata is going to redistribute the potus table into a Spool table so that it can then join the rows to the state table.

With the small sample tables that we created this works very efficient. However if the potus table contained millions of rows, the redistribution could end up being costly.

A join index could be created to get rid of the redistribution problem. Below is the creation SQL for our initial Join Index.

```
create
      join index potus_state_jix as
   select
         p.name, s.state_name
   from potus p join state s on state_id = state_born_id
```

After the Join index is created, let's look at the new EXPLAIN plan that will be used to execute the SQL.

Notice that the base tables are not accessed at all. The Join Index contains all the data that is necessary to fulfill the request. The re-distribution and merge join has been eliminated.

```
select
      name, state_name
from
      potus join state on state_id = state_born_id
3) We do an all-AMPs RETRIEVE step from SYSDBA.POTUS_STATE_JIX by way
   of an all-rows scan with no residual conditions into Spool 1
   (group_amps), which is built locally on the AMPs.  The size of
   Spool 1 is estimated with low confidence to be 8 rows (1,560
   bytes).  The estimated time for this step is 0.03 seconds.
```

Q: As I review the last EXPLAIN plan you presented, Teradata only accessed the join index. So the join index is a physical object. Can I access it directly?
A: To implement any index requires a physical structure and space. A join index is no different. The values are stored in a table structure that Teradata utilizes in the execution of a SQL statement.

Now for the bad news. The Teradata Optimizer has the sole power to determine if a Join Index is going to participate in SQL execution plan. Users can not access the Join Index directly.

Q: In your example, all of the columns you selected were contained in the Join Index. What happens if you select a column that is not part of the Join Index?
A: By now you should know my answer, let's try it and see what happens. We will execute the same SQL as above but add the state _capital column.

```
EXPLAIN select
      name, state_name, state_capital
from
      potus join state on state_id = state_born_id
4) We do an all-AMPs RETRIEVE step from SYSDBA.potus by way of an
   all-rows scan with a condition of ("NOT
   (SYSDBA.potus.state_born_id IS NULL)") into Spool 2 (all_amps),
```

```
     which is redistributed by the hash code of (
     SYSDBA.potus.state_born_id) to all AMPs.  Then we do a SORT to
     order Spool 2 by row hash.  The size of Spool 2 is estimated with
     no confidence to be 13 rows (1,352 bytes).  The estimated time for
     this step is 0.01 seconds.
  5) We do an all-AMPs JOIN step from SYSDBA.state by way of a RowHash
     match scan, which is joined to Spool 2 (Last Use) by way of a
     RowHash match scan.  SYSDBA.state and Spool 2 are joined using a
     merge join, with a join condition of ("SYSDBA.state.state_id =
     state_born_id").  The result goes into Spool 1 (group_amps), which
     is built locally on the AMPs.  The size of Spool 1 is estimated
     with no confidence to be 16 rows (4,512 bytes).  The estimated
     time for this step is 0.05 seconds.
```

As the EXPLAIN plan shows, adding the column not contained in the Join Index caused the Optimizer to ignore the Join Index.

Q: I guess that I just need to include all the columns from the base tables when I create a Join Index. Then I can be confident that it will always be used.
A: That may work but you may run into one of the restrictions of Join Index. A Join Index can only contain 64 columns. In addition, remember the Join Index is basically a table. Filling up the Join Index with rarely used columns can utilize a large amount of space and create poor performance.

Luckily, Teradata allows us to include the ROWID from the base table in the Join Index. This is beneficial when columns from the base table needs to be accessed. In the create Join Index SQL below, we have added the ROWID from the state table into the join index.

```
create
        join index potus_state_rowid_jix as
    select
            p.name, s.state_name, s.ROWID
    from potus p join state s on state_id = state_born_id
```

Now if we generate an EXPLAIN plan for the same SQL that previously ignored the Join Index we observe that it now uses the new Join Index

```
EXPLAIN select
        name, state_name, state_capital
from
        potus join state on state_id = state_born_id
  4) We do an all-AMPs RETRIEVE step from SYSDBA.POTUS_STATE_ROWID_JIX
     by way of an all-rows scan with no residual conditions into Spool
     2 (all_amps), which is redistributed by the hash code of (
     SYSDBA.POTUS_STATE_ROWID_JIX.Field_1027) to all AMPs.  Then we do
     a SORT to order Spool 2 by the sort key in spool field1.  The size
     of Spool 2 is estimated with low confidence to be 8 rows (1,576
     bytes).  The estimated time for this step is 0.01 seconds.
  5) We do an all-AMPs JOIN step from Spool 2 (Last Use) by way of an
     all-rows scan, which is joined to SYSDBA.state by way of an
     all-rows scan with no residual conditions.  Spool 2 and
     SYSDBA.state are joined using a row id join, with a join condition
     of ("Field_1 = SYSDBA.state.ROWID").  The result goes into Spool 1
     (group_amps), which is built locally on the AMPs.  The size of
     Spool 1 is estimated with index join confidence to be 8 rows (
     2,256 bytes).  The estimated time for this step is 0.05 seconds.
```

In Step 4 of the EXPLAIN, it shows that the name and state_name columns are retrieved from the Join Index and placed into a Spool file. This is exactly the same as we saw before we included the state_capital column.

An additional operation, detailed in Step 5, is required to go back to the base state table to retrieve the state_capital column. The ROWID column we included in the Join Index provides the ability to accomplish this.

Q: You mentioned that a Join Index is stored in a table structure. Remembering that Teradata tables are always distributed across the AMPs, are Join Index tables distributed differently?
A: No, the data from Join Indexes are distributed exactly like regular tables. Like a regular table, every Join Index has a Primary Index. In our example so far we have let Teradata default to using the first column as the primary index.

However, when you create a Join Index you can specify specifically what column will be utilized as the Primary Index.

Here we create a Join Index where we include the state_id from the state table and specify that as the Primary Index for the Join Index.

```
create
        join index potus_state_pi_jix as
    select
           p.name, s.state_name, s.state_id
    from potus p join state s on state_id = state_born_id
PRIMARY INDEX (state_id)
```

Q: I created this Join Index and then just for fun generated an EXPLAIN plan for the previous SQL. While it did not contain the ROWID, it still used the Join Index. I thought you said we needed the ROWID for Teradata to be able to go back to the base tables and access data.
A: Ok, a little half truth but I am impressed you went ahead and experimented on your own. Looking at the EXPLAIN plan you received we can indeed see the new Join Index will be used.

```
EXPLAIN select
        name, state_name, state_capital
from
        potus join state on state_id = state_born_id
4) We do an all-AMPs JOIN step from SYSDBA.state by way of a RowHash
   match scan with no residual conditions, which is joined to
   SYSDBA.POTUS_STATE_PI_JIX by way of a RowHash match scan with no
   residual conditions.  SYSDBA.state and SYSDBA.POTUS_STATE_PI_JIX
   are joined using a merge join.  The result goes into Spool 1
   (group_amps), which is built locally on the AMPs.  The size of
   Spool 1 is estimated with low confidence to be 8 rows (2,256
   bytes).  The estimated time for this step is 0.04 seconds.
```

In this case the Join Index contains the UPI of the state table. Since that is also the Primary Index of the Join Index, we know all the data required for the Join will be on the same AMP. Teradata can simply join the Join Index table back to the state table and generate the necessary result set.

This is a perfect example of the Optimizer being smart and evaluating all possible options to find an execution plan that performs optimally.

Q: Besides specifying a different Primary Index for our Join Index are there other table options that a Join Index can take advantage of?
A: Well a powerful feature of Teradata's tables is partitioning and Join Index's can also have Partitioned Primary Indexes.

Let us take a look at an example of a Join Index that utilizes a Partitioned Primary Index.

First let us create some sample tables and populate them with a few values.

```
CREATE table customer_order
      (
      CUSTOMER_ID INTEGER,
      ORDER_DT DATE,
      SHIP_DT DATE,
      DESCRIPTION VARCHAR(1024))
PRIMARY INDEX ( CUSTOMER_ID );

insert into customer_order values
      (1, DATE'2005-01-01', DATE'2005-01-10', 'Stuff');
insert into customer_order values
      (1, DATE'2007-01-01', DATE'2007-01-15', 'Stuff');
insert into customer_order values
      (1, DATE'2008-01-01', DATE'2008-01-25', 'Stuff');

CREATE table customer
      (
      CUSTOMER_ID INTEGER,
      NAME VARCHAR(1024))
PRIMARY INDEX ( CUSTOMER_ID )

insert into customer values (1, 'Walmart');
insert into customer values (2, 'Home Depot');
```

There could be a requirement to query the database and return the description of an item that a specific customer ordered on a specific date. If we created a join index similar to previous examples and looked at the EXPLAIN plan, it would look like:

```
create join index customer_jix as
select
      o.CUSTOMER_ID,
      c.NAME,
      o.ORDER_DT,
      o.DESCRIPTION
from
      customer_order o join customer c on o.customer_id = c.customer_id

exlain
select
      c.NAME,
      o.ORDER_DT,
      o.DESCRIPTION
from
      customer_order o join customer c on o.customer_id = c.customer_id
where
      o.CUSTOMER_ID = 1
```

```
  and o.ORDER_DT = DATE'2007-01-01'
First, we do a single-AMP RETRIEVE step from SYSDBA.CUSTOMER_JIX
by way of the primary index "SYSDBA.CUSTOMER_JIX.CUSTOMER_ID = 1"
with a residual condition of ("(SYSDBA.CUSTOMER_JIX.ORDER_DT =
DATE '2007-01-01') AND (SYSDBA.CUSTOMER_JIX.CUSTOMER_ID = 1)")
into Spool 1 (one-amp), which is built locally on that AMP.  The
size of Spool 1 is estimated with low confidence to be 1 row (717
bytes).  The estimated time for this step is 0.02 seconds.
```

This gives us an efficient single AMP retrieval of our result set. However if the customer_order table contained customers with a large amount of orders the speed of the access could be effected. We have learned while discussing Partitioned Primary Indexes that a PPI may be a good choice.

In our case, since a join is involved we can partition the Join Index and combine the power of the Join Index with the power of partitioning.

In this example we add partitioning to our join creation.

```
create join index customer_order_jix as
select
      o.CUSTOMER_ID,
      c.NAME,
      o.ORDER_DT,
      o.DESCRIPTION
from
      customer_order o join customer c on o.customer_id = c.customer_id
PRIMARY INDEX ( CUSTOMER_ID )
PARTITION BY RANGE_N
    (ORDER_DT  BETWEEN DATE '2003-01-01' AND DATE '2009-12-31'
EACH INTERVAL '1' YEAR , NO RANGE, UNKNOWN)

explain
select
      c.NAME,
      o.ORDER_DT,
      o.DESCRIPTION
from
      customer_order o join customer c on o.customer_id = c.customer_id
where
      o.CUSTOMER_ID = 1
  and o.ORDER_DT = DATE'2007-01-01'
1) First, we do a single-AMP RETRIEVE step from a single partition of
   SYSDBA.CUSTOMER_ORDER_JIX by way of the primary index
   "SYSDBA.CUSTOMER_ORDER_JIX.CUSTOMER_ID = 1,
   SYSDBA.CUSTOMER_ORDER_JIX.ORDER_DT = DATE '2007-01-01'" with a
   residual condition of ("(SYSDBA.CUSTOMER_ORDER_JIX.ORDER_DT = DATE
   '2007-01-01') AND ((SYSDBA.CUSTOMER_ORDER_JIX.CUSTOMER_ID = 1) AND
   (SYSDBA.CUSTOMER_ORDER_JIX.CUSTOMER_ID = 1 ))") into Spool 1
   (one-amp), which is built locally on that AMP.  The size of Spool
   1 is estimated with low confidence to be 1 row (717 bytes).  The
   estimated time for this step is 0.02 seconds.
```

Teradata now will retrieve our data using partition elimination to only have to access a single partition.

Q: That appears to be a very powerful feature. The example however was specifically for accessing data via the order_date. What if I also need to access data on the ship_date column? Do those queries have to suffer performance issues?

A: Nothing prevents us from creating multiple Join Indexes on the same base table. Leaving the customer_order_jix Join Index in place, let us create another join index on the ship_dt column.

```
create join index customer_ship_jix as
select
        o.CUSTOMER_ID,
        c.NAME,
        o.SHIP_DT,
        o.DESCRIPTION
from
        customer_order o join customer c on o.customer_id = c.customer_id
PRIMARY INDEX ( CUSTOMER_ID )
PARTITION BY RANGE_N
        (SHIP_DT  BETWEEN DATE '2003-01-01' AND DATE '2009-12-31'
EACH INTERVAL '1' YEAR , NO RANGE, UNKNOWN)

explain
select
        c.NAME,
        o.SHIP_DT,
        o.DESCRIPTION
from
        customer_order o join customer c on o.customer_id = c.customer_id
where
        o.CUSTOMER_ID = 1
    and o.ship_DT = DATE'2007-01-01'
```

```
1) First, we do a single-AMP RETRIEVE step from a single partition of
   SYSDBA.CUSTOMER_SHIP_JIX by way of the primary index
   "SYSDBA.CUSTOMER_SHIP_JIX.CUSTOMER_ID = 1,
   SYSDBA.CUSTOMER_SHIP_JIX.SHIP_DT = DATE '2007-01-01'" with a
   residual condition of ("(SYSDBA.CUSTOMER_SHIP_JIX.SHIP_DT = DATE
   '2007-01-01') AND ((SYSDBA.CUSTOMER_SHIP_JIX.CUSTOMER_ID = 1) AND
   (SYSDBA.CUSTOMER_SHIP_JIX.CUSTOMER_ID = 1 ))") into Spool 1
   (one-amp), which is built locally on that AMP.  The size of Spool
   1 is estimated with low confidence to be 1 row (717 bytes).  The
   estimated time for this step is 0.02 seconds.
```

In the example, the query looking for items based on order_dt uses the customer_order_jix index and a query based on ship_dt uses the customer_ship_jix index.

Remember that the Teradata optimizer determines which, if any, Join Index will be used. It is important that you verify the execution plan to make sure that the Join Indexes you create are being utilized as you planned.

Q: Are there any other ways in which I can use a Join Index or are they only valuable in instances where you are joining two tables?
A: A Join Index can provide benefits in a number of situations. A Join Index can also be created on a single table.

You may wonder how a Join Index would show any kind of benefit for a single table. A simple example would be to create a Sparse Join Index on a table. Here is an example were we have a table that contains orders that a company receives. The table has the normal order number and description columns. In addition it contains a status column to indicate if the order is still open or it has been completed.

The number of orders this company received is large and the orders are fulfilled quickly. This results in a table with a relatively small number of entries where the status is open ('O') and the majority of the entries closed ('C').

```
create table Orders (
                    order_id integer,
                    description varchar(100),
                    status char(1) )
Primary Index (order_id);

insert into Orders values (1, 'air filter', 'C');
insert into Orders values (2, 'gas filter', 'O');
insert into Orders values (3, 'filter gasket', 'C');
```

It would make sense that this table could be constantly queried to return the open entries. Below is a sample query and the explain plan.

```
select order_id, description, status from Orders where status = 'O'
 3) We do an all-AMPs RETRIEVE step from SYSDBA.Orders by way of an
    all-rows scan with a condition of ("SYSDBA.Orders.status = 'O'")
    into Spool 1 (group_amps), which is built locally on the AMPs.
    The size of Spool 1 is estimated with no confidence to be 1 row (
    61 bytes).  The estimated time for this step is 0.03 seconds.
```

As should be expected an all-AMP retrieve is used that scans the entire table to identify the rows that contain a status = 'O'.

Since we are assuming that this table is extremely large, a lot of resources are used to return a small number of rows.

One way to improve the performance of this query is to create a Join Index on the table. A Join Index is allowed to contain a where clause. By including a where clause on the Join Index we can only include the open rows of the ORDERS table.

```
create Join Index Orders_jix as
   select order_id, description, status from Orders where status = 'O'
```

Now if we examine the EXLAIN plan for the query we see that it uses the Join Index to retrieve the requested result set.

```
select order_id, description, status from Orders where status = 'O'
 2) Next, we lock SYSDBA.ORDERS_JIX for read.
 3) We do an all-AMPs RETRIEVE step from SYSDBA.ORDERS_JIX by way of
    an all-rows scan with no residual conditions into Spool 1
    (group_amps), which is built locally on the AMPs.  The size of
    Spool 1 is estimated with high confidence to be 1 row (61 bytes).
    The estimated time for this step is 0.03 seconds.
```

Q: What am I missing? Yes I can see where the query uses the Join Index but it is still doing an all-AMP retrieve. Isn't that what we were trying to avoid?

A: In our example we are going to have to perform an all-Amp operation. However, the Join Index only contains those rows that are open. All the closed rows have been eliminated in the Join Index. Based on our assumption only a small number of open records exist in the table, we now have a fraction of the disk blocks to scan through.

Q: So Join Indexes help us to increase the performance of our queries when we can pre-join the data or where our query discards a portion of the data. Is this the limit of their magic?

A: After a while, you may get the opinion that there is no limit to the versatility of Join Indexes. If the previously discussed features didn't get you excited about Join Indexes, let's look at another powerful feature.

For this example, our sample table will just have a date and an integer that represents the number of sales that occurred for that day.

We can create this table with the following SQL:

```
create table DailySalesTotals
    (SaleDate      date,
     DailyTotal    integer)
primary index (SaleDate)
```

We insert some data into our newly created table:

```
insert into DailySalesTotals values (date'2008-01-01', 1);
insert into DailySalesTotals values (date'2008-01-15', 1);
                •
                •
insert into DailySalesTotals values (date'2009-04-01', 40);
insert into DailySalesTotals values (date'2009-04-15', 40);
```

Besides using this table to select the number of sales in a specific day, we might want to determine what the total sales were by month. One possible SQL to determine this might be:

```
select
        extract (month from SaleDate),
        extract (year from SaleDate),
        sum(DailyTotal)
from
        DailySalesTotals
group by 1,2
order by 2, 1
```

Now let us take a look at how Teradata is going to execute the query by examining a portion of the resulting EXPLAIN Plan.

```
3) We do an all-AMPs SUM step to aggregate from
   SYSDBA.DailySalesTotals by way of an all-rows scan with no
   residual conditions , grouping by field1 ( EXTRACT(MONTH FROM
   (SYSDBA.DailySalesTotals.SaleDate )) ,EXTRACT(YEAR FROM
   (SYSDBA.DailySalesTotals.SaleDate ))). Aggregate Intermediate
   Results are computed globally, then placed in Spool 3.  The size
   of Spool 3 is estimated with no confidence to be 11 rows (407
   bytes).  The estimated time for this step is 0.05 seconds.
```

Basically, to get the requested results, Teradata is going to read all the rows and sum up their values by month and year. Now as we are thinking about performance, two things should come to mind. First we are doing a full table scan and second we need to do all that arithmetic. If this was a large table, this could be a time consuming and resource intensive task.

What we could do to reduce the impact of this query is to utilize a Join Index. If we were to create a Join Index that pre-aggregates the table, then we could just read the results for the Join Index.

```
create join index DailySalesTotals_jix as
    select
            extract (month from SaleDate) SaleMonth,
            extract (year from SaleDate) SaleYear,
            sum(DailyTotal) MonthlyTotal
    from
            DailySalesTotals
    group by 1,2
```

Examining the EXPLAIN Plan with the Join Index in place we can see that the summations have been eliminated.

```
3) We do an all-AMPs RETRIEVE step from SYSDBA.DAILYSALESTOTALS_JIX
   by way of an all-rows scan with no residual conditions into Spool
   1 (group_amps), which is built locally on the AMPs.  Then we do a
   SORT to order Spool 1 by the sort key in spool field1 (
   SYSDBA.DAILYSALESTOTALS_JIX.Field_1027,
   SYSDBA.DAILYSALESTOTALS_JIX.Field_1026).  The size of Spool 1 is
   estimated with low confidence to be 16 rows (656 bytes).  The
   estimated time for this step is 0.03 seconds.
```

To get the number of sales per month is now a simple scan of the Join Index table to read the results.

Q: Can the Join Index be of any assistance if I need to rollup higher? For example if I needed total sales by year, do I need a separate Join Index for each aggregation I need?
A: Some of that decision will depend on your data and the specific performance requirements for your situation. However, without changing our tables or existing Join Index, let us look at an example of a query and its EXPLAIN Plan rolling up totals by year.

```
EXPLAIN select
        extract (year from SaleDate),
        sum(DailyTotal)
from
        DailySalesTotals
group by 1
order by 1
3) We do an all-AMPs SUM step to aggregate from
   SYSDBA.DAILYSALESTOTALS_JIX by way of an all-rows scan with no
   residual conditions , grouping by field1 (
   SYSDBA.DAILYSALESTOTALS_JIX.Field_1027).  Aggregate Intermediate
   Results are computed globally, then placed in Spool 3.  The size
   of Spool 3 is estimated with no confidence to be 12 rows (348
   bytes).  The estimated time for this step is 0.05 seconds.
```

While the query has to aggregate the values it knows that the Join Index already has the values aggregated by month. So it uses the Join Index to reduce the amount of data that needs to be read and summed.

Hash Indexes.

Q: After all your gushing about Join Indexes, how can HASH Indexes possibly top that? Should I get prepared to be under whelmed?
A: Well maybe a little. A HASH Index is very similar to a single table Join Index and from a functional standpoint provides a sub-set of the Join Index's features. Like Join Indexes, the purpose of a HASH Index is to improve the performance of a SQL query.

Q: So why do we even care about HASH Indexes? If a Join Index can do the same thing why waste the time to learn about Hash Indexes?
A: Good question and since I don't really have a good answer except that a HASH Index may be a little easier to set up and may require a little less space to implement, we will present some simple examples and let you do some independent study.

To perform our investigation of HASH Indexes, we will create a simple table to experiment with.

```
create table candle
    (candle_id integer,
     style_id     integer,
     color        char(25),
     length       integer)
primary index (candle_id)
```

If it was necessary to query the CANDLE table based on the column STYLE_ID a full table scan would be required. This can be seen in the EXPLAIN Plan below:

```
EXPLAIN
  select
        candle_id, style_id, color, length
  from
        candle
  where style_id = '5'
3) We do an all-AMPs RETRIEVE step from SYSDBA.candle by way of an
   all-rows scan with a condition of ("SYSDBA.candle.style_id = 5")
   into Spool 1 (group_amps), which is built locally on the AMPs.
   The size of Spool 1 is estimated with no confidence to be 1 row (
   58 bytes).  The estimated time for this step is 0.03 seconds.
```

To eliminate this all amp scan we could create a HASH Index on the table.

```
create hash index candle_hix
    (style_id, color, length)
on
    candle by (style_id)
order by hash
    (style_id)
```

If we generate an EXPLAIN Plan for the same SQL as before, we now see that the HASH Index has been utilized to eliminate the full table scan and can directly provide the required results.

```
1) First, we do a single-AMP RETRIEVE step from SYSDBA.CANDLE_HIX by
   way of the primary index "SYSDBA.CANDLE_HIX.style_id = 5" with no
   residual conditions into Spool 1 (one-amp), which is built locally
   on that AMP.  The size of Spool 1 is estimated with low confidence
   to be 1 row (58 bytes).  The estimated time for this step is 0.02
   seconds.
```

Q: You are right; this is very similar to what a Join Index does. Does the HASH Index only help to create an alternative direct path?
A: To answer your question, let's get an EXPLAIN Plan for the same SQL but without the WHERE clause.

```
EXPLAIN select candle_id, style_id, color, length from candle
3) We do an all-AMPs RETRIEVE step from SYSDBA.CANDLE_HIX by way of
   an all-rows scan with no residual conditions into Spool 1
   (group_amps), which is built locally on the AMPs.  The size of
   Spool 1 is estimated with low confidence to be 2 rows (116 bytes).
   The estimated time for this step is 0.03 seconds.
```

Teradata still uses the Join Index to satisfy the query.

Q: Wait a second, I just noticed our query included the column CANDLE_ID but that column was not included in our HASH Index create DDL. How is this possible?
A: Excellent observation. CANDLE_ID is the primary index for the base table. The primary index is always automatically included in the HASH Index.

As a matter of fact, you should never explicitly include the primary index in a HASH Index. It will cause duplication that can make the resulting HASH Index require substantially more space.

Dates and Time

"Perfection is achieved, not when there is nothing more to add, but when there is nothing left to take away"

— *Antoine de Saint-Exupéry, Airman's Odyssey*

Q: So why do you have a separate section just for dates and time? One would assume dealing with dates and times would be pretty standard.
A: I agree that dealing with dates and times is boring; however these objects in Teradata do have a few unique characteristics. This is especially true when compared to Oracle.

Q: Don't hold me in suspense, what are the big differences between Oracle and Teradata?
A: In Oracle you have a single data type DATE. The object contains both a date component and a time component in the same object. In Teradata there are three objects relating to date and time:

- Date
- Time
- TimeStamp

TimeStamp would be equivalent to the DATE datatype in Oracle.

Q: If TimeStamp contains both Date and Time attributes why would I even care about the other datatypes, Date and Time?
A: First there is the issue of space. The Teradata datatypes requires the following number of bytes to store their respective values:

DataType	Size in Bytes
Date	4
Time	6
Time with Time Zone	8
TimeStamp	10
TimeStamp with Time Zone	12

If all you required was a Date value, with no time component, using the DATE datatype reduces the space requirement by 60%. How many times in Oracle did you have to truncate a DATE column because you were not interested in the time component?

Q: Can we please start with something really simple. How do I get the current date? In Oracle I do a "select sysdate from dual". Is there a similar pseudo column?
A: Actually there are three pseudo names that can be used to return the current date/time values.

First, the current date can be retrieved by selecting the value from current_date.

```
select current_date;
Current Date
11/20/2008
```

Similarly, the current time can be obtained from current_time.

```
select current_time;
Current Time(0)
10:59:56 AM
```

And finally, the current date and time are both available by selecting the value from current_timestamp.

```
select current_timestamp;
Current TimeStamp(6)
11/20/2008 10:59:56 AM
```

Q: Ok, now that I can access the current date, what is the easiest way to specify a date or time in a SQL statement?
A: The easiest way to specify a date constant in a SQL statement is to use the DATE operation followed by the date desired in single quotes. However the date specified must be in the default system date format. This is usually YYYY-MM-DD format.

For example:

```
select date'2013-02-01' as MyDay;
MyDay
02/01/2013
```

This also works for time and timestamp values:

```
select time'14:59:00' as MyTime;
MyTime
14:59:00.000
```

```
select timestamp'2013-02-01 14:59:00' as MyTimeStamp;
MyTimeStamp
02/01/2013 14:59:00.000
```

Q: Starting with Dates, how does Teradata internally store a date? More importantly, why would it really matter to me?
A: In addition to helping you achieve Teradata Guru Status, knowing how Teradata internally stores dates can assist you in manipulating date values.

Teradata stores a date as a signed integer. The value of the date is a concatenation of the year, month and day. The layout of this integer value is shown below.

As an example, if we have the date January 1, 2008, converting this to the format above would result in the number +20080101
To mathematically convert a year, month and day into this integer format we would perform the calculation

$$(YYYY * 10000) + (MM * 100) + DD$$

Q: Wait a minute if I execute the SQL "select cast (20080101 as date)" **the date 1/1/3908 is returned. Something is wrong here!**
A: You didn't let me finish. Dates are calculated based on the reference of January 1, 1900. So if we did your same calculation but using the integer value 0101 (need to have a valid month and day) we would get 1/1/1900 returned.

Thus, the final step to converting a date into its internal integer format is to subtract 19000000 from the actual date value. Below is a representation of the process.

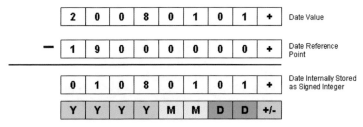

Now if we do a *"select cast (1080101 as date)"* we get the date 1/1/2008 returned.

Q: But what if we want to store a date that is before 1900. Say for example we need to store the value of Sir Isaac Newton's birthday. How would Teradata handle storing the date 1/4/1643?
A: Of course no algorithm could exclude something as important as Sir Isaac Newton's birthday. I think you may have forgotten that the date is stored as a *signed* integer. The mathematics still hold true. The only difference is that we end up with a negative number.

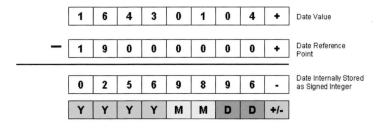

Teradata would store the date as -2569896. Executing the SQL, *"select cast (-2569896 as date)"* would return the correct date.

Q: Back to my previous question, how would this ever help me?
A: Well, let's say you have a date and are only interested in the year value. You could isolate the year by executing the following SQL:

```
select extract (year from DATE'1643-01-04')
```

However, I could also execute this SQL based on the integer arithmetic we previous discussed:

```
select (cast(DATE'1643-01-04' as integer)+19000000)/10000
```

Both SQL's would return 1643.

To return the day from a date we could use the following SQL:

```
select (cast(DATE'1643-01-04' as integer)+19000000) mod 100
```

And finally, the SQL below will get the month value from a date.

```
Select (cast(DATE'1643-01-04' as integer)+19000000) mod 10000/100
```

Q: I cannot believe that the only way to break apart date components is using mathematical formulas. Doesn't Teradata have the concept of the TO_CHAR and TO_DATE functions, like in Oracle?
A: Unfortunately TO_CHAR and TO_DATE are Oracle specific functions. However Teradata does support the ANSI function EXTRACT. The format for the EXTRACT function is:

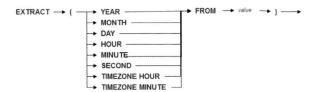

Using the EXTRACT function we could have gotten the same results by executing the following commands

```
select extract (year from DATE'1643-01-04');
Year
1643
select extract (day from DATE'1643-01-04');
Day
4
select extract (month from DATE'1643-01-04');
Month
1
```

Q: I always hated math in school, so why would I want to use your crazy formulas to break apart a date field?
A: The EXTRACT command is a function. Functions require time to set up, pass parameters and return the final result. Extracting the date components

using the mathematical formulas does tend to have a slight performance advantage.

However, you are correct that using the EXTRACT function does make your SQL more understandable and portable.

Q: OK, so now I understand what needs to be done to break apart the components of a date. What if I wanted to display the date in a different format, say January 4, 1663?

A: The CAST command provides the ability to change the format and data type of a date variable. For example, to change our birthday to the format you wanted we could use the following SQL.

```
select cast(cast(DATE'1643-01-04' as format 'M4bDD,bY4') as varchar(100))
1643-01-04
January 04, 1643
```

Q: Wait a second. Why do you need the two CAST functions? I thought that the inter CAST statement would be enough. I executed the following command in "Teradata SQL Assistant".

```
select cast(DATE'1643-01-04' as format 'M4bDD,bY4')
1643-01-04
1/4/1643
```

However, what was displayed was the date still in the default format.

A: Remember we talked about this before when we were formatting numeric values. It is the same ODBC issue. Teradata did reformat the date as you specified but the data type remained as DATE. When the results were returned the ODBC driver formatted the result based on the default format for a DATE.

We need to have Teradata also change the data type to be a string to see the results we were expecting.

Q: What can I say, I forgot! Thanks for reminding me. What about the weird formatting codes? What other formats are available?

A: Below is a chart with the formatting codes that are available for DATE and TIME data fields when converting to a character string.

Date Format Codes	
MMMM or M4	Fully spelled month name. i.e. January
MMM or M3	Abbreviated month name. i.e. Jan
MM	Two digit number of the month. i.e. 01
DDD or D3	Number of days from beginning of year. i.e. January 15 would return 15
DD	Two digit number of the day. i.e. 23
YYYY or Y4	Four digit representation of the year. i.e. 2013
YY	Two digit representation of the year. i.e. 13
EEEE or E4	Full descriptive name for the day of the week. i.e. Thursday
EEE or E3	Abbreviated name for day of the week. i.e. Mon

Valid Date Separators

slash	blank	comma	apostrophe	Colon
/	B or b	,	'	:

period	dash	Decimal digit	Zero Suppressed Digit
.	-	9	Z

Time Format Codes	
HH	Two digit representation of the hour of the day
MI	Two digit representation of the minute of the day
SS	Two digit representation of the second of the day
S(n) or S(F)	Fractional seconds. n can be 1-6 for precision. F precision from data definition
D	Radix symbol.
T	Time to be displayed in 12 hour format.
Z	Time zone displacement. Format +/-HH:MI

Valid Time Separators						
colon	blank	period	dash	hour	minute	second
:	B or b	.	'	h	m	S

Q: Nice chart. These code strings always confuse me. How about a few samples?
A: No problem. Below are a couple of examples of different ways of formatting the current date.

```
select cast(cast(current_date as format 'MMMMbDD,bYYYY') as varchar(100)) as "Result";
Result
November 22, 2013
```

```
select cast(cast(current_date as format 'DDD/YY') as varchar(100)) as "Day of Result";
Result
326/13
```

```
select cast(cast(current_date as format 'DD-MMM-YYYY') as varchar(100)) as "Result";
Result
22-Nov-2013
```

```
select cast(cast(current_date as format 'EEEE,bM4bDD,bYYYY') as varchar(100)) as
"Result";
Result
Friday, November 22, 2013
```

Q: In addition to how dates are represented, manipulating date values and formatting dates, any additional useful information concerning dates I should be familiar with?
A: Teradata provides a very useful function for incrementing a date by month. The ADD_MONTHS function takes two arguments. The first argument is a date value and the second argument is how many months to increase or decrease that date.

In the first example we increment the current date by two months. In the second example we decrement the current date by 20 months.

```
select current_date, add_months(current_date, 2)
Current Date   ADD_MONTHS(Current Date, 2)
11/22/2013     01/22/2014
```

```
select current_date, add_months(current_date, -20)
Current Date   ADD_MONTHS(Current Date, -20)
11/22/2013     03/22/2012
```

Q: What about other date values? For example if I need to know what week of the year a specific date falls in. Do I need to dig out my mathematics books to remember how to do the calculations?

A: While the review session wouldn't kill you, Teradata will save you from missing your favorite TV show. Within the CALENDAR database Teradata provides a view CALENDAR that contains many of the commonly used date calculable values.

The available columns in the CALENDAR view include:

calendar_date	day_of_week	day_of_month	day_of_year
day_of_calendar	weekday_of_month	week_of_month	week_of_year
week_of_calendar	month_of_quarter	month_of_year	month_of_calendar
quarter_of_year	quarter_of_calendar	year_of_calendar	

So to be able to answer your date question, you could use the following SQL.

```
select
      week_of_year
from
      sys_calendar.calendar
where
      calendar_date = current_date
week_of_year
46
```

Q: Now that you have totally overwhelmed me with information about dates, do I even dare to inquire about TIME now?
A: Come on, it is not all that bad. A TIME data type takes 6 bytes to store time values. These 6 bytes are broken down into 3 separate fields.

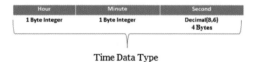

Hour	Minute	Second
1 Byte Integer	1 Byte Integer	Decimal(8,6) 4 Bytes

Time Data Type

In the previous chart containing descriptions for EXTRACT and formatting of DATE included the options available for time.

Q: How about a few formatting example?
A: Happy to oblige. Below are a few examples for formatting time vaues.

```
select cast(cast(current_time as format 'HH:MI:SS') as varchar(100)) as
"Result";
Result
11:23:24
```

```
select cast(cast(current_time as format 'HH:MI:SS.S(3)') as varchar(100))
as "Result";
Result
11:23:24.000
```

```
select cast(cast(current_time as format 'HHhbMImbSSs') as varchar(100)) as
"Result";
Result
11h 23m 24s
```

```
select cast(cast(current_time as format 'HH:MI:SSbT') as varchar(100)) as
"Result";
```

```
Result
11:23:24 AM
```

```
select cast(cast(current_time as format 'HH:MI:SSbZ') as varchar(100)) as
"Result";
```

```
Result
11:23:24 +00:00
```

Q: I would guess that a timestamp is just a combination of a date and time data types?

A: Not exacty. Shown below is the layout for a timestamp variable.

Year	Month	Day	Hour	Minute	Second
2 Byte Integer	1 Byte Integer	1 Byte Integer	1 Byte Integer	1 Byte Integer	Decimal(8,6) 4 Bytes

Timestamp Data Type

Q: When working with timestamps, how would I be able to do a range selection based on hour? For example, if I wanted all the records for a date between 1 am and 8 am.

A: There are a number of ways to accomplish this, below is an interesting example of using the CAST function to create the timestamp range boundaries. In this example, we convert the current date into a string and then concatenate a time string to it. We then use another CAST to transform it into a timestamp data type.

The TimeStampTable is a table that was created with a single timestamp column named TSTAMP. The table was then populated with a row for each hour of the day.

```
select
      count(*) as "Result"
from
      TimeStampTable
where
      tstamp between cast(cast(cast(current_date as format 'YYYY-MM-DD')
as
                          varchar(100)) || ' 01:00:00' as timestamp)
  and                 cast(cast(cast(current_date as format 'YYYY-MM-DD')
as
                          varchar(100)) || ' 08:00:00' as timestamp)
```

```
Result
8
```

This concept can be useful for generating a specific timestamp value.

Functions, Macros and Stored Procedures

"While knowledge can create problems, it is not through ignorance that we can solve them"

— Isaac Asimov

Teradata Internal Functions

Q: I know that it is probably the Math geek in me, but I really love functions. It sure makes writing SQL easier. So how vast is the Teradata library of functions?
A: You may in in for a bit of disappointment. The standard library of functions provided by Teradata is much smaller than is available from many other databases such as Oracle or SQL Server. However, you should be able to find the critical functions you require.

Q: In the chapter on Dates and Time didn't we already utilize Teradata internal functions in those examples?
A: Exactly. Teradata provides a set of functions for retrieving the current date and time information. To recap what we already have seen, The Date and Time internal functions include:

Date and Time Functions		
Function Name	**Description**	**Sample Data Returned**
CURRENT_DATE or DATE	Returns the current date	12/18/2009
CURRENT_TIME or TIME	Returns the current time	10:39:38.000
CURRENT_TIMESTAMP	Returns the current date and time	12/18/2009 10:40:28.000

Q: I normally like to develop a library of utility SQLs that I can use to dump information from the database. To make these scripts as flexable as possible, I often need to know what account I am logged in as. What functions are available to provide system information?
A: Teradata provides a set of functions for exactly that purpose. These system functions include the the ability to obtain the following information:

System Functions		
Function Name	**Description**	**Sample Data Returned**
ACCOUNT	Returns the users current account string	$H_&H
DATABASE	Returns the current user's default database.	SYSDBA
PROFILE	Returns the current users profile (null if none)	DBAPROFILE
ROLE	Returns the user's current role.	DBAROLE
SESSION	Returns the session number for the current user	1000
USER	Returns the current user name string	SYSDBA

Q: How about a quick and simple example using these functions?
A: No problem. Here is a simple SQL statement that displays the account name, current database and session number associated with the user that executes it.

```
Select
        'You are logged in as ' || USER ||
        '. Current Database is ' || DATABASE ||
        '. Session Number is ' || SESSION as SystemInfo
SystemInfo
You are logged in as SYSDBA. Current Database is SYSDBA. Session Number is
1010
```

These functions are also useful when combined with Data Dictionary tables. The Data Dictionary views will be covered in a later chapter.

Q: String manipulation functions are most likely going to be the most important to have available for most of the SQL statements that I will be developing. I am assuming the basic string functions have been implemented.
A: Don't panic. Teradata supports the critical string manipulation fuctions you will probably require. The chart below details the available string functions.

String Functions		
Function Name	**Description**	**Sample Usage**
Concatenation Operator	Returns the combination of two strings. String1 || String2	`select 'abc' || 'xyz'` `abcxyz`
CHAR2HEXINT	Returns a hexidecimal string representing the character string parameter.	`select CHAR2HEXINT('ok')` `006F006B`
INDEX	Returns the starting position of a substring within a string. Returns 0 if substring not found. INDEX(string, substr)	`select INDEX('mystring', 'ring');` `5`
LOWER	Returns the parameter string with all the alpha characters as lower case.	`select LOWER('AB2c4XYX');` `ab2c4xyx`
POSITION	Same as INDEX function. Returns the starting position of a substring within a string. Returns 0 if substring not found. POSITION(subsr in string)	`select POSITION('ring' in 'mystring');` `5`
SOUNDEX	Returns the SOUNDEX code for the string parameter provided.	`Select    SOUNDEX('Teradata');` `T633`
SUBSTRING	Returns a portion of the parameter string SUNSTRING(string FROM n FOR n)	`select SUBSTRING ('Teradata' FROM 5 FOR 4);` `data`

| SUBSTR | Same as SUBSTRING function. Returns a portion of the parameter string SUBSTR(string, start, length) | ```
select
  SUBSTR('Teradata', 5, 4);

data
``` |
| TRIM | Returns a string with the leading and/or trailing character specified removed | ```
select trim(both '.'
  from '..XYX..')

XYX
``` |
| UPPER | Returns the parameter string with all the alpha characters as upper case. | ```
select UPPER('ab2C4xyz');

AB2C4XYZ
``` |
| CHARACTERS | Returns the length of a string | ```
select
  characters('ABCDEF')

6
``` |

Here is an example of a SQL statement that uses string concatenation and trim functions to generate a set of SQL statements to count the rows in tables that were created a specified day.

```
Select
    'select count(*) from ' ||
    trim(DatabaseName) || '.' ||
    trim(TableName) || '; ' as CountSQL
from
    dbc.tables
where
    TableKind = 'T'
  and CreateTimeStamp = DATE'2009-08-31'
CountSQL
select count(*) from DBC.Hosts;
select count(*) from SYSLIB.demddl;
select count(*) from DBC.ResUsageSpdsk;
select count(*) from SYSLIB.dempart;
select count(*) from DBC.Dependency;
....... Partial Display of Returned Rows
```

Q: It appears the important string manipulation functions are available. So what about mathematical functions?

A: Here are the available arithmetic functions in Teradata.

Arithmetic Functions		
Function Name	**Description**	**Sample Usage**
| ABS | Returns the absolute value for the numeric parameter specified. | ```
select abs(-123.12)

123.12
``` |
| CASE_N | Evaluates a list of expressions and returns an index of the first expression that is true. If all expressions are false, null is returned. | ```
select case_n(
  'A' = 'B',
  1 = 2,
  'X' = 'X')

3
``` |
| EXP | Returns the natural logarithm to the power of the value specified. | ```
select exp(1)

2.71828182845905
``` |
| LN | Returns the natural | ```
Select
``` |

	logarithm of the value specified.	`ln(2.71828182845905)`
		
		`1`

LOG	Returns the base 10 logarithm of the value specified.	`select log(100)`
		
		`2`

RANDOM	Returns a random integer. RANDOM(lower, upper)	`select random(1, 100)`
		
		`47`

RANGE_N	Evaluates an expression and returns the position in a list of ranges.	`select range_n(15`
		`  between 1, 10,`
		`  20 ,30 and *)`
		
		`2`

SQRT	Returns the square root for the numeric parameter specified.	`select sqrt(25)`
		
		`5`

ZEROIFNULL	Returns a zero if the parameter passed is equal to null	`select`
		`ZEROIFNULL(null)`
		
		`0`

Q: The offerings do seem to be a little thin. Do I have any options available if I need a specific function that Teradata does not support?
A: Teradata has the ablity for users to write and deploy their own custom functions. The functions are usually written in C and can then be made available from within Teradata. These functions are refered to as UDF (user defined function).

A UDF library of functions implementing a collection of popular Oracle functions has been developed. This library is especially useful if you are converting a number of existing Oracle SQL statements to Teradata.

Search for "Teradata UDFs for popular Oracle functions" using your favorite Web search page. You should be able to locate a link to a download of the functions on the "Teradata Developer Exchange".

Teradata Macros

Q: I do not believe that I have ever seen a database object called a "MACRO". What does it do and why would it hold any interest for me?
A: A MACRO is a Teradata database object that lets you group a number of SQL statements together and then execute them. It is especially useful for tasks that must be performed repetitively or for tasks with complex logic.

A Teradata MACRO is stored in the data dictionary of the database so it can be shared among users. Users can be granted the right to execute the MACRO but prevented from seeing or changing the underlying code. A MACRO can also provide the ability to isolate and limit access of secure tables.

Q: So how do I create one of these MACRO things?
A: Teradata provides a "CREATE MACRO" SQL statement for creating a MACRO. In its simplest form after the CREATE MACRO declaration we simply include SQL statements enclosed in parentheses.

Q: That seems a little vague. Can you give me an example of a MACRO in action?
A: An excellent suggestion! For a super simple example, we will create a MACRO that selects everything from the population table. Below is the SQL syntax to create the MACRO:

```
Create MACRO myMacro as (
    select * from CarClub where CarYear = 2011; );
```

To invoke the MACRO we use the EXECUTE SQL command. When we execute the MACRO the results from the SQL query are displayed.

```
execute myMacro;
Car_id  CarYear  CarMake    CarOwner
3956    2011     MINI       Adams
4017    2011     Cadillac   Perez
795     2011     Jeep       Taylor
387     2011                Scott
1651    2011     Chrysler
• • •
```

Q: When you said simple you really meant simple. How could this be beneficial?
A: I agree, our example is a very simple select statement. However, it could just as well been a complex SQL. The need might arise where a number of users need to execute a complex SQL that a developer devised. Using a MACRO they could retrieve the results without having to know or understand the actual SQL.

Another feature that MACROs provide is the ability to pass parameters. Using the original simple MACRO we could add a parameter to allow us to select the CarYear when the MACRO is executed. The parameters are defined as part of the MACRO name. When referencing the parameters within the MACRO, we just prefix the parameter name with a semi-colon.

```
Create MACRO myMacroParam(inCarYear integer) as (
    select * from CarClub where CarYear = :inCarYear; );
```

Now when we go to execute the MACRO we can pass a value for CarYear to specify what should be retrieved.

```
execute myMacroParam(2012);
Car_id  CarYear  CarMake      CarOwner
1060    2012     Ford         Ramirez
856     2012                  Brown
2589    2012     Land Rover   Green
1304    2012     MINI         Ramirez
3058    2012     RAM          Gonzales
• • •
```

Q: You have started to pique some interest in these MACROs. Can I include multiple SQL statements in the MACRO?

A: Yes, indeed and you are not limited to just SELECT SQL statements. SELECT, UPDATE, INSERT and DELETE statements can all be included in a MACRO definition.

We have here an example of a MACRO that inserts a row into the CarDailyCount table. The row contains the current date and count of the number of rows in the CarClub table. After the row is inserted, a select is performed to display the rows in the CarDailyCount table;

```
Create MACRO myMacroCount as (
      insert into CarDailyCount select date, count(*) cnt from CarClub;
      select * from CarDailyCount order by CountDate desc;);
```

Executing the MACRO it inserts a new row for today's date and then displays the table's data.

```
execute myMacroCount;
CountDate   MemberCarCount
2013-12-19        5000
2013-12-18        4500
2013-12-17        4000
2013-12-16        3500
```

Q: I can see where this would be very useful for database maintenance scripts. Is there any possibility I would be able to include DDL statements within the MACRO?
A: Actually you are in luck, sort of. A DDL statement can be included in a MACRO but it must be the only statement in the MACRO definition.

While this example doesn't make a lot of sense from a practical standpoint, let's say we wanted to include the table create statement for CarDailyCount as part of the MACRO. In addition, after the daily row was inserted, we wanted to drop the table.

Our MACRO might look something like:

```
Create MACRO myMacroCountDDL as (
      create table CarDailyCount(CountDate date, MemberCarCount integer);
      insert into CarDailyCount select date, count(*) cnt from CarClub;
      select * from CarDailyCount order by CountDate desc;
      drop table CarDailyCount;   );
```

However when we tried to execute the statement and create the MACRO we would get an error.

```
*** Failure 3576 Data definition not valid unless solitary.
```

Q: While your example is a little contrived, I could envision wanting to set up a script that would create a table, perform some data manipulation and then clean up after itself. If it was a large table definition with complex processing, I could see an excellent argument for implementing the process using MACROs. Any way this is possible?
A : One possible method would be to place the DDL in separate MACROs and then execute the three MACROs separately.

Below we create two separate MACROs to contain the create table and drop table DDL statements.

```
Replace MACRO myMacroCountCreate as (
     create table CarDailyCount(CountDate date, MemberCarCount integer);
);

Create MACRO myMacroCountDrop as (drop table CarDailyCount ;);
```

Executing the MACROs in sequence provides the desired results.

```
execute myMacroCountCreate;
*** Table has been created.
```

```
execute myMacroCount;
 *** Insert completed. One row added.

CountDate  MemberCarCount
---------  ---------------
 13/12/19            5000
```

```
execute myMacroCountDrop;
*** Table has been dropped.
```

While not an ideal solution, it does allow you to utilize the MACRO functionality to store the required SQL in the database and allow for a simplified execution.

Q: I assume there is a DROP command to delete MACROs that are no longer required?
A: Definitely. If you just need to make a change to the MACRO you can use the REPLACE MACRO statement.

```
Replace MACRO myMacroCountCreate as (
     create table CarDailyCount(CountDate date, MemberCarCount integer);
);
```

The syntax is the same as the CREATE MACRO command except the MACRO must already exist.

If you just want to remove the MACRO entirely the DROP MACRO statement will remove the definition from the database.

```
drop macro myMacroCountCreate;
```

Just be careful, once a MACRO is dropped, there is no way to recover it. It is a good practice to execute a SHOW MACRO command prior to dropping the MACRO and save it to a local disk file.

```
show macro myMacroCount;
Create MACRO myMacroCount as (
     insert into CarDailyCount select date, count(*) cnt from CarClub;
     select * from CarDailyCount order by CountDate desc;);
```

Teradata Stored Procedures

Q: When doing development on my Oracle database, I utilize quite a number of PL/SQL stored procedures. Does Teradata provide the ability to create stored procedures?
A: Yes, Teradata supports the normal database stored procedure object. As in Oracle and other databases Stored Procedures can be very useful in implementing complex operations.

To show a simple example, here is a Stored Procedure to convert a Fahrenheit temperature into a Celsius temperature.

```
create Procedure ConvertToCelsius(in fahrenheit float, out celsius float)
   begin
        declare ConversionFactor float;

        set ConversionFactor = cast (5.0 as float) / cast(9.0 as float);
        set celsius = (fahrenheit - 32.0) * ConversionFactor;
   end;
```

To execute a Stored Procedure in Teradata we use the CALL statement. To find out what the Celsius temperature is for 80 degrees in Fahrenheit we can simply execute the prodedure.

```
call ConvertToCelsius(80, celsius)
celsius
26.67
```

Q: The specific syntax looks a different but the basic structure is similar to what I am familiar to. Do I have access to all the normal conditional and looping constructs?
A: Of course. Let's look at another example that utilizes some of those constructs. In this example we will create a Stored Procedure that populates a table with a specified number of rows. Our CUSTOMERS table will be defined to have only 2 columns.

```
create table Customers (customer_id integer, OrdersThisYear integer)
```

The Stored Procedure will accept the number of rows to create as an input parameter. The customer_id column will start at 1000 and be incremented by 1 for each row. The OrdersThisYear column will vary between the values of 1 and 2.

```
create procedure PopulateCustomers(in TotalItems integer)
begin
     declare customer_id integer;
     declare orders integer;
     declare cnt integer;

     set customer_id = 1000;
     set orders = 1;
     set cnt = 0;

     while (cnt < TotalItems) do
                if (orders > 2) then
```

```
                set orders = 1;
            end if;
            insert into customers values (:customer_id, :orders);
            set cnt = cnt + 1;
            set customer_id = customer_id + 1;
            set orders = orders + 1;
        end while;
end;
```

After the Stored Procedure is called we can examine the rows created;

```
call PopulateCustomers(7);

select * from customers order by customer_id
customer_id   OrdersThisYear
1000          1
1001          2
1002          1
1003          2
1004          1
1005          2
1006          1
```

Q: Is it possible to create a stored Procedure that returns a result set?

A: Yes, not only can your Stored Procedure be written to return a result set; it can return multiple result sets.

In the following example the phrase "dynamic result sets 1" specifies how many result sets the Stored Proedure is going to return. In our example we will return a single result set.

A cursor is defined to create the result set and then we just have to open the cursor.

```
create procedure ReturnResultSet ()
    dynamic result sets 1
begin
    declare ResultCursor cursor with return only for
        select * from customers order by customer_id;

    open ResultCursor;
end;
```

Executing the Stored Procedure displays the rows from our CUSTOMERS table.

```
call ReturnResultSet ();
customer_id   OrdersThisYear
1000          1
1001          2
1002          1
1003          2
1004          1
1005          2
1006          1
```

Q: How are errors handled in a Teradata Stored Procedure?

A: We need to set up a routine to handle what to do if an error occurs, similar to most modern processing languages,.

Here we have a very simple Stored Procedure that divides 2 integers and returns the result.

```
create procedure Divide2Integers (in num integer,
                                  in den integer,
                                  out answer integer )
begin
     declare r integer;

     set r = num / den;

     set answer = r;

end;
```

This works great unless we pass a value of zero as the den parameter.

```
call Divide2Integers (4, 0, answer);
Divide2Integers:Invalid calculation:  division by zero.
```

To prevent the error from happening, we could create an EXCEPTION HANDLER to catch divide by zero errors and just return a zero.

The format for the EXCEPTION HANDLER is:

Adding the EXCEPTION HANDLER to the Stored Procedure now traps the error, assigns a zero for the result and lets the procedure complete without an error.

```
replace procedure Divide2Integers (in num integer,
                                   in den integer,
                                   out answer integer )
begin
     declare r integer;
     declare CONTINUE handler for SQLSTATE '22012'
        set r = 0;

     set r = num / den;

     set answer = r;

end;
```

Running the Stored Procedure now handles the error in the way we designed.

```
call Divide2Integers (4, 0, answer);
answer
0
```

Q: The process makes sense but what is the SQLSTATE '22012' phrase? I am guessing that is the error code for divide by zero but where how do I know that?

A: I agree that it is a cryptic method for specifying exception codes. In the Teradata documentation there is a section specifically on "Mapping Teradata Database Error Messages to SQLSTATE Values".
SQLSTATE is a 5 character string that conforms to ANSI definations.

Q: What if I just wanted to create an EXCEPTION HANDLER that handles any error that may occur?
A: The constant SQLEXCEPTION can be used to accomplish exactly that function. Here we modified our Divide2Integers procedure to set the result to zero no matter what error might be encountered.

```
replace procedure Divide2Integers (in num integer,
                                   in den integer,
                                   out answer integer )
begin
    declare r integer;
    declare CONTINUE handler for SQLEXCEPTION
       set r = 0;

    set r = num / den;

    set answer = r;

end;
```

Q: Are there any downsides to using Stored Procedures in Teradata?
A: Stored Procedures are powerful database constructs that can be extremely beneficial in our processing environment. Also, Stored Procedures are executed in a sequential manor. This step by step iteration makes it easier for us to design a method to accomplish a processing requirement.

However, sequential processing does not lend itself to the parallel processing that makes Teradata so powerful. Many times implementing a solution with a SQL construct will result in a much more efficient and faster solution. The SQL solution may be more difficult to design and implement but the results can be worth the effort.

There are a lot more features available within a Teradata Stored Procedure. Refer to the Teradata documentation for more in-depth information.

Transactions and Security

Transactions and Locking

Q: When I access data in a Teradata table what do I have to be concerned about regarding table locks?
A: The good news is that Teradata handles locking automatically. For user initiated SQL, Teradata utilized three locks: WRITE, READ and ACCESS.

An additional lock type of EXCLUSIVE is used by the database, normally for DDL functions.

Q: A WRITE and READ lock is pretty intuitive but how does an ACCESS lock work?
A: Unlike Oracle, Teradata does not have the concept of a read consistent image. The old Oracle mantra of "Readers don't block writers and writers don't block readers" does not apply in Teradata.

If one session is performing a write, that transaction will block any other session from reading the data until the write transaction completes.

In order to demonstrate this locking behavior we need to control when a transaction is committed. Normally when working in Teradata Mode, a SQL is implicitly committed when it is executed. However, we can use "BEGIN TRANSACTION" and "END TRANSACTION" commands to control when the transaction commit occurs.

Below we have two sessions connected to Teradata. The first session executes a "BEGIN TRANSACTION" and then tries to delete a specific row from the CarClub table.

Before we end the transaction on Session 1, Session 2 attempts to select the same row. Session 2 hangs because Session 1 has the row locked.

Once we execute the "END TRANSACTION" of Session 1, the lock is released and the SELECT from Session 2 can proceed.

The amount of time that is shown for the Session 2 SQL to complete includes the time waiting for the lock to be released.

The default locking mechanism used for a SELECT statement is a READ lock.

Session	SQL Statement

1	`begin transaction;`
	
	`*** Begin transaction accepted.`
	`*** Total elapsed time was 1 second.`
	
	`delete CarClub where Car_id=850;`
	
	`*** Delete completed. One row removed.`
	`*** Total elapsed time was 1 second.`

2	`Select * from CarClub where Car_Id=850;`
	
	`*** Session Hanging ***`

1	`end transaction;`
	
	`*** End transaction accepted.`
	`*** Total elapsed time was 1 second.`

2	`*** Query completed. No rows found.` `*** Total elapsed time was 4 minutes and 31 seconds.`

Now we execute the same set of SQL commands but instead add a "LOCK ROW FOR ACCESS" clause on the select statement. From the example we can see that the Session 2 SELECT immediately returns the "No rows found" result.

Session	SQL Statement

1	`begin transaction;`
	
	`*** Begin transaction accepted.`
	`*** Total elapsed time was 1 second.`
	
	`delete CarClub where Car_id=850;`
	
	`*** Delete completed. One row removed.`
	`*** Total elapsed time was 1 second.`

2	`lock row for access select * from CarClub where Car_id=557;`
	
	`*** Query completed. No rows found.`
	`*** Total elapsed time was 1 second.`

1	`end transaction;`
	
	`*** End transaction accepted.`
	`*** Total elapsed time was 1 second.`

An ACCESS lock performs a dirty read. In this case we received a "No rows found" result. However, if after Session 2 received the result, Session 1 performed a ROLLBACK and then an "END TRANSACTION" we would have received an incorrect result.

Q: The concept of a READ lock and an ACCESS lock is still a little confusing. I understand what you described about Dirty Reads and that a READ could have to wait for a WRITE to complete but READs by themselves shouldn't cause any concerns, correct?
A: To maybe better understand how a READ lock occurs, we can reverse the previous example.

In this case we execute our BEGIN TRANSACTION statement and then issue a select for a specific row. The data for that row is returned and displayed as we would suspect.

If Session 2, now tries to delete the same row, the DELETE statement hangs. Even though Session 1 was only doing a read, the READ lock prevents the delete from proceeding.

Once the "END TRANSACTION" statement is executed, the READ lock is released and the DELETE statement completes.

Session	SQL Statement

1	`begin transaction;`
	
	`*** Begin transaction accepted.`
	`*** Total elapsed time was 1 second.`
	
	`Select * from CarClub where Car_Id=663;`
	
	`*** Query completed. One row found. 4 columns returned.`
	`*** Total elapsed time was 1 second.`
	
	`    Car_id    CarYear CarMake`
	`----------- ----------- ------------------------------------------`
	`       663        2009 McLaren`

2	`delete CarClub where Car_id = 663;`
	
	`*** Session Hanging ***`

1	`end transaction;`
	
	`*** End transaction accepted.`
	`*** Total elapsed time was 1 second.`

2	`*** Delete completed. One row removed.` `*** Total elapsed time was 2 minutes and 29 seconds.`

What could present an unacceptable issue is that a SELECT transaction could lock a row preventing a delaying completion of load or update process.

Q: Wow, I am thinking that this could be a real issue. A mischievous user could really wreak havoc with data loading processes?
A: That is why it is a "Best Practice" to always have users access tables via a view. An excellent architectural layout out would be to create one database for the data tables and another for views that refer to those tables.

Application users would then be directed to access the table's data from the view database. This organization could follow something similar to what is detailed below.

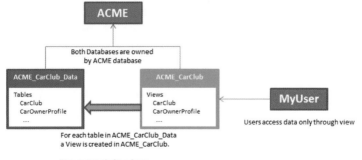

When creating the "base table views" an ACCESS locking clause could be included in the view definition to prevent users from row locking data in the table.

```
REPLACE VIEW "ACME_CarClub"."CarClub"(
     Car_id
    ,CarYear
    ,CarMake
    ,CarOwner
) AS
LOCKING ROW for Access
SELECT
     Car_id
    ,CarYear
    ,CarMake
    ,CarOwner
FROM "ACME_CarClub_DATA"."CarClub";
```

Privileges

Q: I like the concept but what prevents the users from just accessing the data directly from the table database?
A: Like most modern databases, Teradata provides the ability to grant access rights on database objects.

Users could only be granted rights on the view database and no rights on the data database.

Below is a simplified view of the GRANT SQL command for granting rights on database objects.

A nice option is that you can grant a privilege on an entire database/user account with a since SQL command. For example, to grant myUser select access on all the objects within the ACME_CarClub database we could use the following statement.

```
grant select on ACME_CarClub to myUser;
```

Since we set up our database design to separate the views and tables it can make the access maintenance easier.

Q: I thought I had everything down. First, I set up accounts like in your example. Then created a sample table in ACME_CarClub_DATA and base table view in ACNE_CarClub. After executing the GRANT you showed above, I figured I need to also

grant privileges for ACME_CarClub to be able to select from ACME_CarClub_DATA so I executed the statement:

```
grant select on ACME_CarClub_DATA to ACME_CarClub
```

However, when I logged into myUser and tried to select data from ACNE_CarClub.CarClub I get the error:

```
An owner referenced by user does not have SELECT WITH GRANT OPTION access
to ACME_CarClub_DATA.CarClub.Car_id.
```

Q:What is this "with grant option" thing?
A: Good work taking the initiative to try and finish up setting up our sample design. My fault for not giving you all the information you were going to require. However, in my defense, I did say the syntax diagram was a partial view of the GRANT command.

Giving the view database, ACME_CarClub access to ACME_CarClub_DATA only extends to that database.

So we were trying to access a view in ACME_CarClub that then in turn needed to access the table in ACME_CarClub_DATA. ACME_CarClub needs the ability to extend his right to access ACME_CarClub_DATA to other users or databases that have rights on his objects.

The "with grant option" provides the ability to grant this privilege. What you need to execute is:

```
grant select on ACME_CarClub_DATA to ACME_CarClub with grant option
```

Q: Much better. Now I can see the data?
A: It does take a little bit of work to set things up and diligence to keep the databases clean but in the long run will make user maintenance easier to bear.

Roles

Q: Is there anything else that can assist with the whole privilege maintenance nightmare? While I agree that careful design of the database structure can make it easier, in a complicated installation it could get messy quickly.
A: Teradata provides for the ability to create roles. A role can be defined and then privileges can be assigned to that role. The role can then be granted to an individual user.

In that manner, a change to access rights can be applied to the role and all the users with that role will automatically be granted the new privilege.

Q: How would you go about defining a role and implementing it?

A: It is actually very simple. First we need to create the role. The SQL below will create a role which we can use for read only users.

```
Create role ACME_CarClub_ReadOnly;
```

Now privileges can be assigned to the role instead of directly to an individual user. The role can then be granted to each user that requires the privileges the role owns.

```
grant select on ACME_CarClub to ACME_CarClub_ReadOnly;

grant ACME_CarClub_ReadOnly to myUser;
```

The user myUser can now access ACME_CarClub just like if he was directly assigned the rights directly.

Teradata Data Dictionary

> "Usually its users discover sooner or later that their program does not deliver all the desired results, or worse, that the results requested were not the ones really needed."
>
> — *Niklaus Wirth*

Database and User Information

Q: Interspersed in this Teradata journey of enlightenment, you have referenced and shown SQL examples of extracting information from the database itself. What additional tidbits of knowledge can you share?

A: Whatever database you are working, being familiar with the data dictionary can prove to be invaluable. Teradata stores all the information that is required for the database to function correctly. This includes all of the object, view and index definitions, assigned privileges, role and profile assignments in addition to a treasure chest of information.

One of the first places to start pursuing the Data Dictionary is to examine the data stored concerning Database and User Information.

Most of the Data Dictionary information is available via views in DBC. The primary view we can use for Database and User information is contained in the DBC.DATABASES view. The full view description is included in the Appendix.

In this example we will query the DBC.DATABASES view to retrieve some basic information about the databases that exist.

```
select DatabaseName, CreatorName, OwnerName, DBKind from dbc.databases
DatabaseName    CreatorName   OwnerName   DBKind
TDPUSER         DBC           DBC         U
SQLJ            DBC           DBC         D
financial       DBC           Samples     D
SysAdmin        DBC           DBC         U
manufacturing   DBC           Samples     D
   • • •
```

Q: This can be useful information to see if a database or user exists in the database. Quick question; what is the DBKind column for?

A: Remember in Teradata there are two types of database accounts, user accounts and database accounts. The DBKind column indicates what type of account the entry is. A value of "U" in the DBKind column indicates the DatabaseName is a User account and a value of "D" indicates a database account.

Q: I looking at the available columns in the DBC.DATABASES view, I see columns referring to PermSpace, SpoolSpace and TempSpace. Is this the amount of space that account is currently using?

A: No, in the database view the amount of space you are allocated is what is available.

We can simply select the space allocation from the view to determine what allocations these space assignments have been assigned for an account.

```
select
      DatabaseName,
      PermSpace / 1024 / 1024 as "PermSpace(Mbytes)",
      SpoolSpace / 1024 / 1024 as "SpoolSpace(Mbytes)",
      TempSpace / 1024 / 1024 as "TempSpace(Mbytes)"
from
      dbc.databases
where
      databasename in 'sysdba'
```

DatabaseName	PermSpace(Mbytes)	SpoolSpace(Mbytes)	TempSpace(Mbytes)
sysDBA	100	1024	1024

Q: I notice that there is also a DBC.USERS view. If the DBC.DATABASES view shows information for both database and user accounts, why do we need a USERS view?
A: The DBC.USERS view only has entries for accounts defined as user accounts. While these same accounts also have entries in DBC.DATABASES, the users view adds additional information that is associated with connecting to the database. For example when the password was last modified or a startup string that should be executed upon logon is detailed in the DBC.USERS table.

```
select
      UserName, PasswordLastModDate, PasswordLastModTime
from
      dbc.users
where
      UserName = 'sysdba'
```

UserName	PasswordLastModDate	PasswordLastModTime
sysDBA	11/22/2013	11:36:57.000

Object Information

Q: What about information concerning database objects, such as TABLES, VIEWS, MACROS etc.?
A: The main view we will want to look at is the DBC.TABLES view. One might assume based on the view name, that this view contained information just about tables. It does, however also contains data on all of the Teradata database objects.

Similar to the DBKind column in the DBC.DATABASES view, the DBC.TABLES view contains a TableKind column that specifies what type of object the item refers to. The TableKind column is a single alphabetic character which defines the objects as indicated below:

A	Aggregate function		B	Combined aggregate and ordered analytical function
D	JAR		E	External Stored Procedure
F	Standard function		G	Trigger
H	Instance or Constructor Method		I	Join Index
J	Journal		M	Macro
N	Hash Index		O	No Primary Index
P	SQL Procedure		Q	Queue Table
R	Table function		S	Ordered analytical function
T	Table		U	User-defined data type
V	View		X	Authorization
Y	GLOP Set			

Below we search the DBC.TABLES view for a specific object name, 'CarClub' that is owned by the database 'sysDBA'. In this instance, in addition to the DatabaseName, we display the TableKind code and the SQL text that was used to create the object. Referencing the TableKind list above, we can determine that the 'CarClub' object is indeed a table.

```
select
      DatabaseName, TableKind, RequestText
from
      dbc.tables
where
      databasename = 'sysDBA' and tablename = 'CarClub'
```

DatabaseName	TableKind	RequestText
sysDBA	T	CREATE TABLE CarClub (Car_id INT , ...

The layout of the DBC.TABLES view in the appendix details all of the valuable information that is available in this view.

Q: That is kind of weird naming, You would have thought Teradata would have called it something like DBC.OBJECTS or something. The view does provide an excellent source for object and specifically table information, but what about more in-depth information. Where can I find information concerning the columns of a table?
A: The DBC.COLUMNS view can be queried to see the columns that make up a table definition. In this example, we display the columns and some of the column's properties that make up the 'CarClub' table.

```
select
      ColumnName, ColumnType, ColumnLength, Nullable
from
      dbc.columns
where
      databasename = 'sysDBA'
  and tablename = 'CarClub'
order by
      columnId
```

ColumnName	ColumnType	ColumnLength	Nullable
Car_id	I	4	Y
CarYear	I	4	Y
CarMake	CF	100	Y
CarOwner	CV	1024	Y

Q: Here it is again, another set of codes to determine the column data type. Are you going to be nice and list out the code translations again?
A: Well just partially nice. Below is a list of the commonly used ColumnType code translations. For the full list you will have to break down and look it up in the Teradata documentation.

AT	TIME		CF	CHAR
CV	VARCHAR		D	DECIMAL
DA	DATE		F	FLOAT
I1	BYTEINT		I2	SMALLINT
I	INTEGER		TS	TIMESTAMP

Index Information

Q: Continuing on the path of finding table related information, how can I determine what indexes exist on a table?
A: The view you will want to query is the DBC.INDICES view. By querying the view for a specific table and in a database we can see all the indexes that exist for that table.

```
select
        IndexType,
        IndexName,
        ColumnName,
        IndexNumber,
        ColumnPosition
from
        dbc.indices
where
        databasename =  'sysDBA'
    and tablename = 'Vacations'
order by IndexNumber, ColumnPosition
```

IndexType	IndexName	ColumnName	IndexNumber	ColumnPosition
P		VacationId	1	1
S	VacationsNUSI	DepartureDate	4	1
S	Vacations_mcUSI	LocationId	8	1
S	Vacations_mcUSI	DepartureDate	8	2

And yes, before you go crazy, there is an IndexType column whose value needs to be translated in order to determine the type of index.

D	Derived column partition statistics		H	hash ordered ALL covering secondary
I	ordering column of composite secondary index		J	join index
K	primary key		M	Multi-Column Statistics
N	hash index		O	valued ordered ALL covering secondary
P	Nonpartitioned Primary		Q	Partitioned Primary
S	Secondary		U	unique constraint
V	value ordered secondary		1	field1 column of a join or hash index
2	field2 column of a join or hash index			

In our example we have 3 indexes defined on the Vacations table. If an index is defined as containing multiple columns, a row will exist for each column in the index. The IndexNumber column can be used to separate what rows are associated with what indexes. The ColumnPosition column indicates the order of the columns in a multiple column index.

The VacationID column makes up the Primary Index for the Vacations table. In addition, there are 2 additional Secondary Indexes. The DepartureDate column makes up one of the secondary indexes. The final secondary index is defined as both the LocationID and DepartureDate columns.

Space and Sizing Information

Q: How can I determine how much PermSpace I am currently using?

A: Space utilization information can be found in the DBC.DISKSPACE view. To see the amount of PERM space a database is utilizing the query below can be executed.

```
select
      DatabaseName,
      sum(MaxPerm) / 1024 / 1024 as MaxPerm,
      sum(CurrentPerm) / 1024 / 1024 as CurrentPerm,
      (sum(MaxPerm) - sum(CurrentPerm)) / 1024 / 1024 as AvailablePerm
from
      dbc.diskspace
where
      databasename = 'sysDBA'
group by
      DatabaseName
```

DatabaseName	MaxPerm	CurrentPerm	AvailablePerm
sysDBA	100	10.70654296875	89.29345703125

The results indicates that the database sysDBA is correctly using a little over 10 mBytes of storage and has 89 mBytes remaining from his 100 mByte allocation.

Q: Why are we summing the values from DBC.DISKSPACE?
A: Remember that space is allocated to AMPs. The DBC.DISKSPACE view reports the available space by AMP. The column vproc indicates what AMP the row is referring to. By summing all the AMP values together we get the utilization for the entire database.

Without aggregating the values we can see that of the 100 mBytes allocated to sysDBA each of the two AMPs has 50 Mbytes assigned.

```
select
      vproc,
      MaxPerm   / 1024 / 1024 as MaxPerm,
      CurrentPerm   / 1024 / 1024 as CurrentPerm
from
      dbc.diskspace
where
      databasename= 'sysDBA'
order by
      vproc
```

Vproc	MaxPerm	CurrentPerm
0	50	5.35791015625
1	50	5.3486328125

Q: What if I would like to see the space allocations for a specific table? The DBC.DISKSPACE view only seems to have information at the database level.
A: That is true. If we would like to see the space metrics for a specific table we need to look at the DBC.ALLSPACE view. Here space is broken down by table. To look at the space allocation for a specific table we could execute a SQL query such as:

```
select
      vproc,
      TableName,
      CurrentPerm   / 1024 / 1024 as CurrentPerm
from
      dbc.allspace
where
```

```
        databasename= 'sysDBA'
  and   TableName = 'Vacations'
order by
        vproc
Vproc    TableName    CurrentPerm
0        Vacations    1.89208984375
1        Vacations    1.8916015625
```

Q: Looking at the results that were displayed, it appears that the amount of space utilized on each AMP is pretty much the same. Does this mean we have a good distribution for this table?
A: Excellent observation! The DBC.ALLSPACE view can be used to check on how well a Primary Index is performing in regard to data distribution.

To validate this point, we can take the data from the Vacations tables and create a new table where we modify the VacationId column to make all the values the same. This would force Teradata to store all the rows on the same AMP.

If we then looked at the utilization in DBC.ALLSPACE for this table, we can clearly see the poor data distribution across the AMPs.

```
select
        vproc,
        TableName,
        CurrentPerm  / 1024 / 1024 as CurrentPerm
from
        dbc.allspace
where
        databasename= 'sysDBA'
  and   TableName = 'VacationsSkew'
order by
        vproc
Vproc   TableName          CurrentPerm
0       VacationsSkew      1.2109375
1       VacationsSkew      0.0009765625
```

Session Information

Q: Are there any views that will let me see who is currently connected to the database?
A: Yes, the DBC.SESSIONINFO view exists to provide information about the currently active session on the database. We can determine what users are connected to the database, when they logged in and additional information specific to their session.

In this SQL we display information from DBC.SESSIONINFO to list all the current sessions for the sysDBA user.

```
select
        sessionNo,
        UserName,
        LogonDate,
        cast(LogonTime as Varchar(30) )as LogonTime
from
        dbc.SessionInfo
where
        UserName = 'sysDBA'
```

```
order by
      username
SessionNo   UserName   LogonDate    LogonTime
1000        SYSDBA     08/24/2013   09:38:30.47
```

Q: With all these canned applications we utilize, this typed of query can be quite useful in determining if the application is still connected to the database. How about any history of when a user was connected to the database?

A: The DBC.LOGONOFF view can be accessed to create a historical timeline of when a specific user was connected to the database.

```
select
      UserName,
      LogDate,
      cast(logtime as Varchar(30)) as LogTime,
      SessionNo,
      Event
from
      dbc.logonoff
where
      username = 'sysDBA'
  and LogDate between date'2013-08-24' and date'2013-08-26'
order by
      logdate,  logtime
UserName   LogDate      LogTime       SessionNo   Event
SYSDBA     08/24/2013   10:12:57.65   1000        Logon
SYSDBA     08/24/2013   16:51:34.51   1000        Logoff
SYSDBA     08/25/2013   11:09:51.42   1000        Logon
SYSDBA     08/25/2013   14:45:59.98   1001        Logon
SYSDBA     08/25/2013   14:46:34.41   1001        Logoff
.......  Partial Display of Returned Rows
```

Since a single user account may logon on to the database multiple times and their sessions overlap, the SessionNo column is used to identify each unique session.

Final Thoughts

"But where are you going?"

"Oh, I've got the whole universe. Planets to save, civilisations to rescue, creatures to defeat and an awful lot of running to do."

— Jenny, "Dr. Who, Series 4, Episode 6 - The Doctor's Daughter"

Q: This Teradata Indroduction has really helped me get an understanding the Teradata database. I think with all the topics covered, the main lesson I learned is how much I still need to understand.

I think now I can speak some of the Teradata jargon and I actually have grown to appreciate the power and features available in Teradata.

Where can I go from here?
A: I am glad you found the material helpful. Teradata provides unique database architecture that is providing solutions for the ever increasing volume and processing requirements of modern businesses.

To expand you expertise of Teradata, you need to spend as much time as possible working directly with Teradata.

Keep you mind open to new ideas and keep asking questions.

The Internet has a wealth of information relating to Teradata. Let Google be your best friend.

With all of the topics presented here, we only touched the surface. Take areas of interest and dive deeper in the topic to truly get a full understanding.

The first Internet link you should visit is www.teradata.com. In addition to all the product information is a vast array of articles and white papers.

Teradata also publishes a magazine that can provide additional educational articles as well as new product information. You can subscribe at www.teradatamagazine.com.

Appendix – Selected Data Dictionary Views

Included in this appendix are selected DBC views that were referenced in the content of this document.

All of the information was extracted from the Teradata database data dictionary Table and Column comments.

View DBC.ALLSPACE	
The DBC.AllSpace view provides information about disk space allocation and usage. The columns are: Vproc, DatabaseName, AccountName, TableName, MaxPerm, MaxSpool MaxTemp, CurrentPerm, CurrentSpool, CurrentTemp, PeakPerm, PeakSpool and PeakTemp.	
Column Name	Comments
Vproc	The AllSpace.Vproc field identifies the AMP Vproc reporting the space.
DatabaseName	The AllSpace.DatabaseName field identifies a data base or user.
AccountName	The AllSpace.AccountName field identifies an account.
TableName	The AllSpace.TableName field identifies a table within a database.
MaxPerm	The AllSpace.MaxPerm field specifies the permanent space allocated to the data base per AMP.
MaxSpool	The AllSpace.MaxSpool field specifies the maximum amount of spool space per AMP that the user can consume.
MaxTemp	The AllSpace.MaxTemp field specifies the maximum amount of temporary space per AMP that the user can consume.
CurrentPerm	The AllSpace.CurrentPerm field gives the amount of permanent space per AMP currently being used by the data base.
CurrentSpool	The AllSpace.CurrentSpool field gives the amount of spool space per AMP currently being used by the user.
CurrentTemp	The AllSpace.CurrentTemp field gives the amount of temporary space per AMP currently being used by the user.
PeakPerm	The AllSpace.PeakPerm field gives the maximum amount of permanent space per AMP that has been use by the data base since the last time the DBC.ClearPeakDisk macro was run.
PeakSpool	The AllSpace.PeakSpool field gives the maximum amount of spool space per AMP that has been use by the data base since the last time the DBC.ClearPeakDisk macro was run.
PeakTemp	The AllSpace.PeakTemp field gives the maximum amount of temporary space per AMP that has been use by the data base since the last time the DBC.ClearPeakDisk macro was run.
MaxProfileSpool	The AllSpace.MaxProfileSpool field specifies the maximum amount of spool space per AMP that the user can consume as specified by the user's profile spool space setting.
MaxProfileTemp	The AllSpace.MaxProfileTemp field specifies the maximum amount of temporary space per AMP that the user can consume as specified by the user's profile temporary space setting.

VIEW DBC.COLUMNS

Each row of the DBC.Columns view provides information about a table or view column, or a stored procedure or a macro parameter. Some of the column names are: DatabaseName, TableName, ColumnName, ColumnFormat, ColumnTitle, ColumnType, DefaultValue.

Column Name	Comments
DatabaseName	The Columns.DatabaseName field identifies the data base in which the table, view, stored procedure or macro resides.
TableName	The Columns.TableName field identifies the table, view, stored procedure or macro.
ColumnName	The Columns.ColumnName field identifies the column of the table or view, or parameter of the stored procedure or the macro.
ColumnFormat	The Columns.ColumnFormat field specifies the format of column data.
ColumnTitle	The Columns.ColumnTitle field specifies the heading for the column.
SPParameterType	The Columns.SPParameterType specifies the type of the parameter in case of stored procedure object as I (in), O (out) and B (inout).
ColumnType	The Columns.ColumnType field specifies the type of data in a table or view column, or stored procedure or macro parameter as I (integer), F (floating), D (decimal), CF (fixedcharacter), CV (var. character), BF (fixed binary), and BV (var.binary).
ColumnUDTName	The Columns.ColumnUDTName field specifies the name of a UDT if that column data type is a UDT.
ColumnLength	The Columns.ColumnLength field specifies the length of the column in number of characters.
DefaultValue	The Columns.DefaultValue field specifies any default value assigned to the column.
Nullable	The Columns.Nullable field specifies whether the column may contain a null value, as Y (yes) or N (no).
CommentString	The Columns.CommentString field contains any user-supplied text for the column.
DecimalTotalDigits	The Columns.DecimalTotalDigits field contains the total number of digits in a column with type equal to decimal.
DecimalFractionalDigits	The Columns.DecimalFractionalDigits field contains the fractional number of digits in a column with type equal to decimal.
ColumnId	The Columns.ColumnID field contains the internal identifier assigned to the column by the DBC.
UpperCaseFlag	The Columns.UpperCaseFlag field indicates whether the column is to be stored in uppercase and whether comparisons on the column are case specific. U = Uppercase and not specific, N = not uppercase and not specific, C = not uppercase and specific.
Compressible	The Columns.Compressible field contains a C if the column is compressible when it is stored in the DBC.
CompressValue	The column is removed from tvfields so NULL is being returned.
ColumnConstraint	The Columns.ColumnConstraint field contains the condition text for column level Check.
ConstraintCount	The Columns.ConstraintCount field contains the count of table level constraints referencing this column.
CreatorName	
CreateTimeStamp	

LastAlterName	
LastAlterTimeStamp	
CharType	
IdColType	
AccessCount	
LastAccessTimeStamp	
CompressValueList	The Columns.CompressValueList field contains the list of values that will be compressed from the column.

View DBC.DATABASES

Each row of the DBC.Databases view provides information about a data base. The column names are: DatabaseName, CreatorName,   OwnerName, ProtectionType, PermSpace, SpoolSpace, TempSpace and CommentString.

Column Name	Comments
DatabaseName	The Databases.DatabaseName field identifies the data base.
CreatorName	The Databases.CreatorName field identifies the username that created the data base.
OwnerName	The Databases.OwnerName field identifies the data base from which this data base was created.
AccountName	The Databases.AccountName field identifies the account to be charged for the space used by the database.
ProtectionType	The Databases.ProtectionType field specifies the fallback option default for tables created in the data base as Y (yes, fallback is the default) or N (no, nofallback is the default.)
JournalFlag	The Databases.JournalFlag field specifies the default journal options for tables created in the database. The values can be N for None, S for Single and D for Dual. The first character is for before images and the second for afters.
PermSpace	The Databases.PermSpace field specifies the total permanent space in bytes allocated to the data base.
SpoolSpace	The Databases.SpoolSpace field specifies the maximum spool space permitted to the database.
TempSpace	The Databases.TempSpace field specifies the maximum temporary space permitted to the database.
CommentString	The Databases.CommentString field contains any user-supplied text for the data base.
CreateTimeStamp	
LastAlterName	
LastAlterTimeStamp	
DBKind	
AccessCount	
LastAccessTimeStamp	

View DBC.DISKSPACE

The DBC.DiskSpace view provides information about disk space allocation and usage by AMP, database (user) and account. The column names are: Vproc, DatabaseName, AccountName, MaxPerm, MaxSpool, CurrentPerm, CurrentSpool, PeakPerm and PeakSpool.

Column Name	Comments
Vproc	The DiskSpace.Vproc field identifies the AMP Vproc reporting the space.
DatabaseName	The DiskSpace.DatabaseName field identifies a data base or user.
AccountName	The DiskSpace.AccountName field identifies an account.
MaxPerm	The DiskSpace.MaxPerm field specifies the permanent space allocated to the data base per AMP.
MaxSpool	The DiskSpace.MaxSpool field specifies the maximum amount of spool space per AMP that the user can consume.
MaxTemp	The DiskSpace.MaxTemp field specifies the maximum amount of temporary space per AMP that the user can consume.
CurrentPerm	The DiskSpace.CurrentPerm field gives the amount of permanent space per AMP currently being used by the data base.
CurrentSpool	The DiskSpace.CurrentSpool field gives the amount of spool space per AMP currently being used by the user.
CurrentTemp	The DiskSpace.CurrentTemp field gives the amount of temporary space per AMP currently being used by the user.
PeakPerm	The DiskSpace.PeakPerm field gives the maximum amount of permanent space per AMP that has been use by the data base since the last time the DBC.ClearPeakDisk macro was run.
PeakSpool	The DiskSpace.PeakSpool field gives the maximum amount of spool space per AMP that has been use by the data base since the last time the DBC.ClearPeakDisk macro was run.
PeakTemp	The DiskSpace.PeakTemp field gives the maximum amount of temporary space per AMP that has been use by the data base since the last time the DBC.ClearPeakDisk macro was run.
MaxProfileSpool	The DiskSpace.MaxProfileSpool field specifies the maximum amount of spool space per AMP that the user can consume as specified by the user's profile spool space setting.
MaxProfileTemp	The DiskSpace.MaxProfileTemp field specifies the maximum amount of temporary space per AMP that the user can consume as specified by the user's profile temporary space setting.

View DBC.INDICES

The DBC.Indices view provides information about indexes on tables. The column names are: DatabaseName, TableName, IndexNumber, IndexType, UniqueType, IndexName, ColumnName, and ColumnPosition.

Column Name	Comments
DatabaseName	The Indices.DatabaseName field identifies the data base.
TableName	The Indices.TableName field identifies the table on which the index is built.
IndexNumber	The Indices.IndexNumber field gives the internal number assigned to the index.
IndexType	The Indices.IndexType field identifies the index type as P (primary index), S (secondary index), U (unique), K (primary key).
UniqueFlag	The Indices.UniqueFlag field indicates if the index is unique as Y (yes, means unique) or N (no, means non-unique.)
IndexName	The Indices.IndexName field identifies the name of the index.
ColumnName	The Indices.ColumnName field identifies a column of an index.
ColumnPosition	The Indices.ColumnPosition identifies the position of the column within an index.
CreatorName	
CreateTimeStamp	
LastAlterName	
LastAlterTimeStamp	
IndexMode	Indices.IndexMode is H (secondary index rows are hash distributed to the AMPs), L (secondary index rows are on the same AMP as the referenced data row), or NULL (primary index). If the index type is J or N, index mode is L but has no meaning.
AccessCount	
LastAccessTimeStamp	

View DBC.LOGONOFF

The DBC.LogOnOff view provides information about Logon and Logoff events. The column names are: LogDate, LogTime, Username, AccountName, Event, LogicalHostId, IFPNo, SessionNo, LogonDate, LogonTime and LogonSource.

Column Name	Comments
LogDate	The LogOnOff.LogDate field gives the date of the event in the form yy/mm/dd.
LogTime	The LogOnOff.LogTime field gives the time of the event in the form hh:mm:ss.
UserName	The LogOnOff.Username field identifies the user.
AccountName	The LogOnOff.AccountName field identifies an account.
Event	The LogOnOff.Event field identifies the event as: logon (successful), logoff (successful), bad user (unsuccessful logon attempt), bad account (unsuccessful logon attempt), or bad password (unsuccessful logon attempt).
LogicalHostId	The LogOnOff.LogicalHostId field identifies the host from which the event occurred.
IFPNo	The LogOnOff.IFPNo field is the PE Vproc number of the PE to which the session was assigned.
SessionNo	The LogOnOff.SessionNo field is the session number assigned to the user for the logon.
LogonDate	The LogOnOff.LogonDate field is the date that the logon occurred. It is useful for matching the Logoff entry to the Logon entry.
LogonTime	The LogOnOff.LogonTime field is the time that the logon occurred. It is useful for matching the Logoff entry to the Logon entry.
LogonSource	The LogOnOff.LogonSource field is an identification of the place from where the user accessed the system. It may be a host job id, a network address... .

View DBC.ROLEINFO	
The RoleInfo view provides information about roles. The column names are: RoleName, CreatorName, CommentString and CreateTimeStamp.	
Column Name	**Comments**
RoleName	DBC.RoleInfo.RoleName contains the names of roles defined in the database.
CreatorName	DBC.RoleInfo.CreatorName names the user that created a role.
CommentString	DBC.RoleInfo.CommentString contains any user-supplied text for the role.
CreateTimeStamp	DBC.RoleInfo.CreateTimeStamp indicates the date and time a role is created.
ExtRole	DBC.RoleInfo.ExtRole indicates if a role is externally assigned.

View DBC.SESSIONINFO
The DBC.SessionInfo view provides information about current sessions.

Column Name	Comments
UserName	The UserName column contains the name under which the logon occurred.
AccountName	The AccountName column identifies the account that will be charged for the system resources used during the session.
SessionNo	The SessionNo column is the identifier assigned to the session by the TDP or LAN Interface.
DefaultDataBase	The DefaultDatabase column is the name of the database to be associated with the session.
IFPNo	The IFPNo column is PE Vproc number of the PE to which the session was assigned.
Partition	The SessionInfo.Partition field is the task in the DBC that is associated with the session. This is normally DBC/SQL; i.e. the DBC parser.
LogicalHostId	The SessionInfo.LogicalHostId field is the host identifier from which the user is logged on. It contains the host number and the Host format.
HostNo	The SessionInfo.HostNo field is the number of the host from which the user is logged on.
CurrentCollation	The CurrentCollation column represents current collation of the session. It can be E, A, or M for EBCDIC, ASCII or MULTINATIONAL collation correspondingly
LogonDate	The SessionInfo.LogonDate field is the date that the logon for this session occurred.
LogonTime	The SessionInfo.LogonTime field is the time that the logon for this session occurred.
LogonSequenceNo	The SessionInfo.LogonSequenceNo field is the logon sequence number for the session.
LogonSource	The SessionInfo.LogonSource field is an identification of the place from where the user accessed the system. It may be a host job id, a network address... .
ExpiredPassword	
TwoPCMode	A 2 in Column DBC.Sessioninfo.TwoPCMode indicates a 2PC mode session
Transaction_Mode	
CurrentRole	The CurrentRole column contains the user's current role for the session.
ProfileName	The ProfileName column contains the profile assigned to the user.
LogonAcct	The LogonAcct column contains the user's logon account.
LDAP	The LDAP column contains "Y" if the session is LDAP-based, "N" otherwise.
AuditTrailId	The AuditTrailId column is the user identifier that will be used for access logging.
CurIsolationLevel	
QueryBand	The QueryBand column contains the queryband assigned to the session.
ProxyUser	The ProxyUser column contains the name of the proxy user if the session has a proxy connection.
ProxyCurRole	The ProxyCurRole column contains the name of the current proxy role if the session has a proxy connection.

View DBC.TABLES

Each row of the DBC.Tables view provides information about a table, view, stored procedure or macro. The column names are: DatabaseName, TableName, TableKind, CreatorName, ProtectionType, RequestText, CommentString, QueueFlag, CommitOpt and TransLog.

Column Name	Comments
DatabaseName	The Tables.DatabaseName field identifies the data base in which the table, view, stored procedure or macro resides.
TableName	The Tables.TableName field identifies the table, view, stored procedure or macro.
Version	The Tables.Version field is incremented each time the tables structure changes. The DBC/SQL statements which will increment the version are any MODIFY TABLE, CREATE/DROP INDEX and RENAME.
TableKind	The Tables.TableKind field specifies the kind of object as T (table), V (view), P (stored procedure) or M (macro).
ProtectionType	The Tables.ProtectionType specifies the fallback option that was selected for the table as follows: Y (yes, table has fallback) or N (no, table does not have fallback.)
JournalFlag	The Tables.JournalFlag field specifies the journal options for the table as two characters whose values can be N for None, S for Single, and D for Dual. The first character is for before images and the second for afters.
CreatorName	The Tables.CreatorName field identifies the username that created the table, view, stored procedure or macro.
RequestText	The Tables.RequestText field contains the most recent data definition statement for the table, view or macro.
CommentString	The Tables.CommentString field contains any user-supplied text for the table, view, stored procedure or macro.
ParentCount	The Tables.ParentCount field contains the count of the Parent tables for the table.
ChildCount	The Tables.ChildCount field contains the count of the Child tables for the table.
NamedTblCheckCount	The Tables.NamedTblCheckCount field contains the count of named table-level Check constraint for the table.
UnnamedTblCheckExist	The Tables.UnnamedTblCheckExist indicates if the table has unnamed table-level Check constraint: Y (yes, means has) or N (no, means does not have).
PrimaryKeyIndexId	The Tables.PrimaryKeyIndexId identifies the Primary Key index Id for the table. It is NULL if table does not have a Primary Key.
RepStatus	The Tables.RepStatus identifies the replicated table status for the table. It is NULL if the table is not a member of any replication group.
CreateTimeStamp	
LastAlterName	
LastAlterTimeStamp	
RequestTxtOverflow	The Tables.RequestTxtOverFlow identifies that the Request Text for the object has overflown in DBC.TVM and the complete text is stored in DBC.TextTbl.
AccessCount	
LastAccessTimeStamp	
UtilVersion	The Tables.UtilVersion contains the utility version count. This column is modified to match the Version column when a significant change of

	the table definition occurs that would prohibit an incremental restore or copy of an archive.
QueueFlag	The Tables.QueueFlag field specifies the queue option as a single character whose value can be either Y if it is queue table, or N if it is not a queue table.
CommitOpt	The Tables.CommitOpt specifies the ON COMMIT option for a temporary table. Value P stands for ON COMMIT PRESERVE ROWS. Value D stands for ON COMMIT DELETE ROWS. Value N indicates the object is not a temporary table.
TransLog	The Tables.TransLog specifies whether transaction journals will be generated. Value Y means transaction journals will be generated, value N indicates no transaction logging.
CheckOpt	The Tables.CheckOpt indicates if the table allows duplicate rows or not:Y (yes, duplicate rows are allowed for table) or N (no, duplicate rows arenot allowed for table).

View DBC.USERS

Each row of the DBC.Users view provides information about a user. The column names can be obtained by using the HELP VIEW DBC.Users.

Column Name	Comments
UserName	The Users.Username field identifies a user.
CreatorName	The Users.CreatorName field identifies the username that created the user.
PasswordLastModDate	The Users.PasswordLastModDate field gives the Date the Password was last modified.
PasswordLastModTime	The Users.PasswordLastModTime field gives the Time the Password was last modified.
OwnerName	The Users.OwnerName field identifies the data base from which the user was created.
PermSpace	The Users.PermSpace field specifies the total permanent space in bytes allocated to the user.
SpoolSpace	The Users.SpoolSpace field specifies the maximum spool space permitted by the user.
TempSpace	The Users.TempSpace field specifies the maximum temporary space permitted by the user.
ProtectionType	The Users.ProtectionType field specifies the fallback option default for tables created in the user database as Y (yes, means fallback is the default) or (no, means no fallback is the default.)
JournalFlag	The Users.JournalFlag field specifies the default journal options for tables created in the users database. The values can be N for None, S for Single and D for Dual. The first character is for before images and the second for afters.
StartupString	The Users.StartupString field gives the startup string specified for the user.
DefaultAccount	The Users.DefaultAccount field gives the default account for logons and disk space usage.
DefaultDataBase	The Users.DefaultDatabase field gives the default database, if one was ever specified, for logons.
CommentString	The Users.CommentString field contains any user-supplied text for the user.
DefaultCollation	The Users.DefaultCollation field specifies default collation for logons. It can be E, A, M, H for EBCDIC, ASCII, MULTINATIONAL or host collation correspondingly
PasswordChgDate	The Users.PasswordChgDate contains the date on which the current password was assigned to the user. This value is NULL for a new user.
LockedDate	The Users.LockedDate contains the date on which the DBase row was locked to logons due to excessive erroneous passwords.
LockedTime	The Users.LockedTime contains the time formatted HH:MM, at which the DBase row was last locked to logons due to excessive erroneous passwords.
LockedCount	The Users.LockedCount contains the number of successive unsuccessful attempts to logon to the user with an erroneous password.
TimeZoneHour	
TimeZoneMinute	
DefaultDateForm	
CreateTimeStamp	
LastAlterName	
LastAlterTimeStamp	
DefaultCharType	
RoleName	
ProfileName	The Users.ProfileName contains the name of the

	profile assigned to the user. This value is NULL if the user has no profile assigned.
AccessCount	
LastAccessTimeStamp	

Printed in Great Britain
by Amazon